Challenging the Mind, Touching the Heart

This book is dedicated to my two children, Lindsay and Blaise.
Their support of me has been most helpful.
I have learned much about assessment from them.

* * *

INSTRUCTION TOUCHES THE MIND,
ASSESSMENT TOUCHES THE HEART

* * *

The harsh word of criticism flies on eager wings. It requires no skill, any one can be an expert. But it causes bitter resentment wherever it falls. The kind word of correction is far more effective. We accept correction without loss of pride, which is the most sensitive trait we have. However, it is much better to use the magic word of appreciation. Every heart is hungry for appreciation. We double our efforts when someone sees the good in us.

—Captain John V. Noel, U.S. Navy,
Division Officer's Guide (1962)

Challenging the Mind, Touching the Heart

Best Assessment Practices

Robert A. Reineke

CORWIN PRESS, INC.
A Sage Publications Company
Thousand Oaks, California

For information:

Corwin Press, Inc.
A Sage Publications Company
2455 Teller Road
Thousand Oaks, California 91320
E-mail: order@corwin.sagepub.com

SAGE Publications Ltd.
6 Bonhill Street
London EC2A 4PU
United Kingdom

SAGE Publications India Pvt. Ltd.
M-32 Market
Greater Kailash I
New Delhi 110 048 India

Printed in the United States of America

Library of Congress Cataloging-in-Publication Data

Reineke, Robert Arthur.
Challenging the mind, touching the heart : best assessment practices / by Robert A. Reineke.
p. cm.
Includes bibliographical references.
ISBN 0-8039-6630-X (pbk. : acid-free paper). — ISBN 0-8039-6629-6 (cloth : acid-free paper)
1. Educational tests and measurements—United States.
2. Learning. 3. Teaching—United States. I. Title.
LB3051.R3557 1998
371.26—dc21 97-21152

This book is printed on acid-free paper.

98 99 00 01 02 03 04 10 9 8 7 6 5 4 3 2 1

Editorial Assistant: Kristen L. Gibson
Production Editor: Michele Lingre
Production Assistant: Lynn Miata
Typesetter/Designer: Danielle Dillahunt
Cover Designer: Marcia M. Rosenburg

CONTENTS

Preface vi

Acknowledgments x

About the Author xi

How to Use This Book xii

1. Assessment Foundations 1
2. Developing Effective Students 19
3. Creating a Manageable Curriculum 39
4. Using Assessment Information Effectively 58
5. Assessment: The Professional Imperative 87
6. Building a Supportive Assessment Culture 107

Chapter Activities 117

Appendix A: Personal Professional Portfolio 124

Appendix B: Suggested Readings 127

Appendix C: Scoring and Grading 128

Appendix D: Examples of Assessment: Knowing the State Capitals 138

References 140

PREFACE

Childhood, seemingly endless to the young, quickly passes; with it, pass a multitude of opportunities for learning and development. Parents, teachers, and others charged with care and nurturing of the young possess an intuitive sense of the importance of these formative years and recognize the hazard of lost or misplaced opportunity. Understandably, then, the 13 years a child spends in public or private schools convey a sense of urgency and importance.

The report on the status of education in the United States, *A Nation at Risk: The Imperative for Educational Reform*, reflected the urgency and importance of making the most of educational opportunities for young people. Since its publication in 1983, much attention has been focused on what might be done to ensure that the educational opportunities afforded our young people are the best possible. Virtually every education-related organization in the country has spent considerable effort examining the problem and has offered remedies in the form of programs, plans, and new models for education. These efforts should continue. But a central premise of this book is that change in practice will occur only when endorsed and practiced in the classroom where learning occurs—teachers interacting with students. One area that holds considerable promise to improve learning opportunities for students is assessment.[1]

This book is designed to help educators consider how assessment relates to instruction and recognize how assessment affects student learning. In particular, the message of this book is to encourage teachers to review their assessment practices and establish an assessment climate in which students can safely seek and use assessment information. A basic assumption is that learning best occurs in a positive setting, one in which students can develop competence and build self-confidence and one that treats "mistakes" as a normal but temporary condition.

As this book deals with the two primary tools for teaching and learning, namely instruction and assessment, it is especially critical for teachers; their assessment practices directly impact students. But other educators, including members of boards of education, superintendents, principals, and those who support the professional growth of education professionals, can enhance their capability to support teachers in developing effective classroom practices. They are in positions to support the classroom climates and school cultures essential to effective assessment practices that promote student learning.

Those in the best position to choose or develop assessment methods are classroom teachers. Assessment is an integral part of instruction; effective assessment is essential for student learning. At the same time, professional obligation requires that teachers seek new and better approaches for their work—that is, that they assess their own instruction. The most effective approach for improving instruction and assessment is for teachers, in conjunction with colleagues, to develop assessment strategies that best address their instructional goals and their students' needs.

A dominant message is that effective assessment is an instructional issue rather than a technical one. Effective classroom assessment does not require the technically sophisticated procedures that attend formal testing such as national standardized tests. But effective assessment practices do require that teachers weigh the benefits and limitations of various assessment methods and ensure that they are useful for students. The assessment perspective presented in this book is based on assessment experiences common to everyone.

This book does not address the important question of selection; nor is it intended to be critical of standardized achievement tests or tests designed for purposes other than learning. Decisions that result in admitting one student but not another to a prestigious university are difficult at best. As critical as these decisions are, it is important that we not lose sight of the purpose of schools as institutions of learning. Standardized tests were developed with the good intention of reducing bias in judgment and thereby promoting equal opportunity for all students. At the same time, legitimate questions arise as to whether these tests reflect desired educational outcomes and whether their use in schools enhances students' opportunity to learn. Errors in the selection process that deny opportunities to deserving students are indeed grave; we need to keep them to an absolute minimum. Important questions and issues regarding selection need to be addressed, but not here.

The ideas in this book follow from the fundamental belief that the purpose of schooling is to promote student competence in the curriculum. To achieve this purpose, five interdependent elements are discussed: effective students, a meaningful curriculum, useful assessment information, a professional staff posture, and a supportive work environment. Effective schools are those where effective students pursue competence in a meaningful curriculum that becomes known to them through useful instruction and assessment orchestrated by professional educators, all of which requires adequate administrative and community support.

The opening chapter describes assessment for learning as different from assessment used for other purposes. Ten assessment principles and five dimensions of assessment information are offered, as well as a general process to review assessment practices. The principles and assessment dimensions serve as a framework to guide the development of effective assessment practices.

The second chapter suggests that effective students, in particular students who seek and use assessment information, are indispensable for effective schools. Students are the major users of assessment information and can also serve as valuable assessment resources. Developing students' capacity to produce and use assessment information contributes to their effectiveness as learners and adds to the efficiency of the assessment process. This chapter outlines characteristics of effective students and suggests areas, such as the assessment climate, that help students use assessment information.

The third chapter reminds us that a meaningful curriculum along with effective instruction and assessment lead to high-quality work. The suggestion is made to streamline the curriculum and place more emphasis on developing skills, a sense of understanding, and high-quality work. A manageable curriculum helps students do work of high quality and achieve a sense of personal competence. The more relaxed instructional pace that accompanies a leaner curriculum is beneficial in part because it expands possibilities for assessment procedures and use of an assessment strategy directed at student competence in valued knowledge and skills.

Chapter 4 extends the discussion of assessment practices to information use. A major point here is that the principal criterion for choosing appropriate assessment procedures is assessment purpose. Assessment for learning first and foremost serves students and teachers. Assessment information must promote learning. Because assessment information for learning is for student use, the way it is given is important.

Chapter 5 extends the idea that effective assessment serves professional educators as well as students. Assessment practices and criteria that help effective students are also useful for the professional educator; effective assessment practices are as critical for educators as they are for students. The premise for the chapter is that teachers seek to expand their professional skills and build confidence in them. The message is that effective and enduring professional growth occurs as professional teachers build effective practices, based on their strengths, through cooperative efforts and collegial exchange. Professional growth embodies assessment principles congruent with and complementary to effective assessment of students.

Finally, Chapter 6 addresses the crucial issue of the support needed to help educators review their instruction and assessment practices. In addition to time and resources, professional teachers need and deserve a supportive work culture. A culture that encourages teachers to give and receive useful information promotes their professional growth and contributes to their professional well-being. In particular, a supportive culture helps teachers experience the personal rewards that attend effective teaching. Questions or worksheets for each chapter are included at the end of the book to help readers clarify their assessment beliefs, examine their assessment purposes, and guide their development of effective assessment practices.

A major point of this book is to offer an assessment perspective that connects assessment with instruction and learning. Assessment for learning requires teaching professionals to consider their practices in terms such as the impact assessment has on students, the power of assessment, the intimate connection between assessment and instruction, and the support needed to alter assessment practice. Based on a fundamental belief in educators as professionals, this book deals with attitudes, values, and assessment strategies that address student learning. It is my hope that readers will gain appreciation of the pervasive nature of assessment and feel encouraged to expand their repertoire of assessment strategies by building on their own experience. Finally, an important message is that professional educators benefit from talking with one another about their craft. I hope that this book will stimulate such collegial discussions.

Notes

1. In this book, I make a distinction between assessment and testing. In doing so, I suggest that assessment reflects a more comprehensive set of activities and methods to promote learning than does testing. Evaluation is an acceptable alternative but carries connotations that might get in the way of my purposes here.

ROBERT A. REINEKE

Acknowledgments

At some time in our life, many of us are fortunate enough to encounter at least one individual who touches us in a very positive way. In most cases, these people knew how to assess our performance in a way that caused us to seek their counsel. To my good fortune, I encountered many such individuals. A number of these individuals, but not all, are mentioned below.

I am indebted to all the teachers and others who did not give up on me; who preserved my sense of "able" in spite of performance lapses; who helped me develop a sense of quality, even if it was not always achieved; who introduced the value of questions, not simply answers; and who sensitively assessed my performances in ways that were constructive and useful.

I owe a great deal to the Navy flight instructors and fellow student pilots who lived performance assessment with me. Their concern for my welfare and confidence in me contributed to my appreciation of effective assessment—as well as my longevity. My interest in assessment as well as my writing this book is as much due to my experiences in flight training as to my professional training and experience in measurement and evaluation.

My parents showed a special confidence in me—they rarely interfered in my pursuits but believed that I would succeed. Less-than-stellar performances in school were always greeted with "You could do better if you wanted to."

Several individuals made helpful suggestions during the writing of this book. I thankfully acknowledge the contributions of Sharon Cirone, De Ann Currin, Kathy Ewers, Arlen Gullickson, Joanna Petz, Jennifer Petz, and Greg Sandstrom. I am also appreciative of the encouragement received from students in my graduate classes on classroom assessment. My editors, Alice Foster and Michele Lingre, and copyeditor, Stephanie Hoppe, provided many helpful suggestions in guiding the development and production of this work. My wife, Jackie, not only reviewed the manuscript and offered many comments and suggestions but encouraged and inspired me throughout the writing process. Her support was invaluable.

About the Author

Robert A. Reineke is an evaluation specialist for Lincoln Public Schools and Adjunct Associate Professor at the University of Nebraska, Lincoln. He has a bachelor's degree in psychology and a doctorate in educational psychology, both from the University of Minnesota. He has taught graduate courses in classroom assessment and consulted with school districts regarding assessment issues. In the 6 years between his degree programs, he was a naval aviator and staff officer in the U.S. Navy. His assessment perspectives have been influenced by 20 years of experience in assessment-related work.

How to Use This Book

Following the last chapter are suggested discussion questions and activities that will help you establish effective assessment practices. As you progress through this book, you will find recurrent themes, such as attributes of assessment information or assessment as a process. Consequently, some of you may want to read the entire book before beginning the chapter activities; others of you may benefit from completing them as you go along. Either way, carrying out these activities will result in an active document to guide your assessment practices, help you develop your assessment skills, identify resources to help you create and carry out an effective assessment plan, and amplify the personal and professional rewards that attend teaching.

Appendix A outlines components of a personal professional portfolio, particularly as they relate to assessment practices. You may find it helpful to use this portfolio outline as you respond to questions or complete suggestions activities associated with each chapter. The activities and portfolio outline are offered as general guides only; altering them to suit your needs and style is encouraged. I also suggest that you invite a colleague or create a study group to discuss assessment issues, build a supportive assessment climate, and collectively review and refine assessment practices. The "best" instructional practices are likely to result when professional teachers talk with one another about their craft.

The assessment perspective described here treats assessment as a process, not a procedure. Gaining facility in the process will take time. I encourage you to proceed at a deliberate pace, but not hurry. Professionally guided review of instruction and assessment practices involves some personal risk. A trusted colleague or friend is a valuable asset for this process. When looking for ways to strengthen your professional skills, do not lose sight of your strengths or the magnitude of your task.

1

ASSESSMENT FOUNDATIONS

"Instruction touches the mind;
assessment touches the heart."

Assessment of student performance is a current topic and, I hope, also an enduring one. Attention to this essential element of instruction is long overdue. As controversy continues about which assessment methods are best, the number of teacher workshops that speak to "new" assessment methods and teacher education programs that offer courses in classroom assessment increases. Individuals and groups concerned with improving education or critical of the quality of education in the United States have generated much of the recent interest in assessment. Proponents touting alternative assessment strategies see them as better than current ones. Education critics, on the other hand, frequently suggest a need to improve test scores, especially on national, standardized tests. These critics stress the importance of comparing test scores of current students with past students or students in the United States with students from other countries.

Students, like their adult counterparts, are concerned about comparisons, but students compare their performance with that of peers. In addition to national examinations, results from classroom tests and other schoolwork provide quantitative student performance indicators that establish course grades and attendant class rank. Test scores, grades, and class rank profoundly affect students during and at the conclusion of their school experience.

Emphasis on test scores and the idea of raising them are relatively new phenomena in education. Throughout the 20th century, there has been a gradual shift in assessment emphasis from learning and competency to selection and accountability. This shift in emphasis represents a departure of monumental proportions from the historical basis of education and training.

Similarly, it represents a substantial departure from the educational heritage on which this country was founded, namely, education for an informed citizenry and to build individual competence and know-how. The traditional value of schooling appears to have changed from getting an education to getting selected.

Some relevant questions have arisen from the echo of exhortations to examine and raise test scores of U.S. students. What does current practice in instruction and assessment suggest we want students to know and what do we want our students to be able to do? How does assessment impact what students learn? How does assessment help students learn? What do test scores mean? What is classroom assessment about and what should classroom assessment be about? These questions suggest that student knowledge and performance are primary instructional issues, test scores are not, and that student learning deserves increasing attention over concerns regarding accountability or selection. Taking this perspective, a number of individuals have suggested that both instruction and assessment need overhauling and have offered new programs and procedures, including alternative ways to assess students.

Educators increasingly face questions about their assessment practices: Do they rely on multiple choice or short answer tests or have they adopted the "new" methods currently touted as being superior for determining what students know and can do? As a result, many school districts are changing or considering changing the way they test students, often turning to "new" assessments such as authentic assessment, performance assessment, and portfolios.

It is common to hear people reverse the distinction between old and new when referring to assessment methods. "New" assessment practices, such as portfolios and performance assessments, are really older than the multiple choice tests commonly found in today's classrooms; clearly they are much older than the machine-scored versions of multiple-choice tests. Perhaps efforts to revive older assessment methods signal a return to a more traditional education philosophy—that is, that schools should help students become competent in reading, writing, mathematics, the sciences, and the humanities.

The tension between assessment information to promote student competence and assessments that provide summary scores to serve selection and accountability decisions continues. Given that it is likely that this tension will remain, the challenge for educators is to assess students in ways that best serve their needs. As a practical matter, we need to weigh the value of assessment information that nurtures student competence with test scores that quantify competence or compare competence levels between students and create assessment practices that strike an effective balance between the two assessment outcomes.

It is instructive to consider the value of test scores. What information do they convey to students? How do scores contribute to students' knowledge and competence? How do scores impact students? Test scores, as overall performance summaries, are useful in establishing quantitative indicators that allow comparisons between performances; such indicators serve information needs external to the student. Most of us would agree, however, that students need information about how their performances compare to some known standards if they are to confirm their skill or know what they need to do to improve. From a learning perspective, assessment information must either affirm competence or provide guidance about what students can do to achieve it. Information and affirmation powerfully impact learning. Walberg (1984), in his synthesis of research, concluded that of 27 instructional quality and time effect variables, reinforcement for correct performance has the most positive effect on learning, whereas cues and feedback ranked fourth in impact. Wiggins (1993) devotes an entire chapter to the subject of feedback. He writes, "A score on a test is encoded information; feedback is information that provides the performer with direct, usable insights into current performance, based on tangible differences between current performance and hoped-for performance" (p. 182). Finally, Gullickson (1993) writes about the singular focus on providing assessment information to the teacher, who then channels it to students. He notes that one undesirable effect of this is to build a dependency between student and teacher that encourages student reliance on the teacher to do the evaluative thinking so essential to the learning process.

Connecting Assessment With Learning

Providing assessment information to students and helping them use such information is a recurrent theme of assessment for learning. One implication of this perspective is that criteria and standards for assessments that address student learning are far different than for assessments that serve other purposes. Efficient scoring, for example, a strength of multiple-choice tests, has value when the purpose of assessment is to assign grades or compare performances of large numbers of students. Scoring efficiency achieved by limiting assessment information to a summary score such as percentage correct does not, however, best serve student learning. Multiple-choice tests remain useful in classrooms, but their value for students depends on the information they provide, not their ease of scoring.

Performance assessments, portfolios, multiple response formats, essays, and short answer tests are all potentially effective assessment tools. These tools become effective when educators think carefully about the context, conditions, and purposes for using them. It is appropriate that teachers make decisions about classroom assessment. To ensure that assessment practices are effective, educators—especially teachers—need the skills to purposefully devise or select assessment strategies. A key part of developing effective assessments is to align them with beliefs and goals regarding instruction and learning. Establishing beliefs and goals precedes developing specific assessment procedures. A major point of this book is to offer an assessment perspective that once again connects assessment with learning.

The Power of Assessment

A second point is to remind us that the assessment process itself includes powerful elements. Awareness of these elements is crucial to making sound decisions about effective assessment. The assessment context and climate, characteristics of the learner, and the purpose of instruction are all relevant to instructional effectiveness for students, both individually and collectively. In other words, students' experience with assessment influences their learning as much as the instruction they receive.

Critique is at the heart of the learning process. The character of criticism, its manner of delivery, and individuals' receptivity to it become important for learning, both in adults and students. Everyone, to a greater or lesser degree, is tense or anxious when faced with the judgment of others; such feelings commonly attend public speaking, performance anxiety, and test anxiety. Every individual, child and adult alike, carries assessment "baggage" that serves to frame current criticism. This baggage may include incidents of ridicule by peers, too quickly offered or repeatedly negative reactions by parents, laughter at a closely held idea, or receiving a C– or "Do over" in response to an essay written with great effort. For many, the degree of anxiety that surrounds the receipt of assessment information reaches a debilitating level.

Some students seek to avoid the negative impact of criticism through compulsive perfectionism. These individuals attempt to stave off any hint of personal failure by pleasing the would-be judge, be it parent, teacher, or peer; they color between the lines. Another means for escape is to withdraw from the judgment process altogether, either emotionally—"I didn't study for this test"—or physically, by dropping out of school. These reactions insulate individuals from the fear or pain of negative judgments by persons having real or perceived power over them.

The assessment climate that students experience profoundly influences their attitudes and behavior in school and thus becomes a critical factor for learning. Students, particularly those with negative school experiences, are highly sensitive to the conditions that attend assessment of their performance. For such students, the assessment process itself is painful and therefore one to be avoided. Given the importance of assessment information for learning, students who avoid assessment place themselves at a severe disadvantage. Learning involves personal risk. Individuals seek personal competence; assessment tells them whether they are competent or not. Risking the effort necessary to learn can spring from the expectation to succeed, but taking that risk also requires the capacity to fail. Both are important learner characteristics. Students who lack one or both of these attributes may develop debilitating patterns of behavior that limit their capacity for learning.

Students doing marginal work are not the only ones with limited capacity to risk learning. Consider the issue of course selection. Students, often with perfect or near-perfect grade point averages, may avoid difficult courses or teachers who "grade hard." Presumably, these students perceive failure as receiving a grade other than an A. There are striking similarities between students who avoid classes and thereby avoid the possibility of negative assessment and those who avoid assessment altogether by dropping out of school. The personal and emotional nature of assessment impacts all students.

Competence and Confidence

The primary goals of schooling and hence the purposes of instruction and assessment are to promote students' sense of personal competence and confidence. Effective assessment is essential for attaining both goals. Personal competence is experienced by achieving something that is complete, such as tying a shoe or reading a book. It is the successful culmination to a learning experience. Pursuit of competence is what characterizes the young child, the effective student, and the professional teacher. Children and adults alike seek independence and validation through personal competence. Individuals often develop competence solely through independent practice and self-assessment. In schools, however, competence develops through instruction and assessment that applies to performances or knowledge structures as defined by the curriculum. For the most part, teachers are responsible for assessment of skill development and knowledge.

Competence begins with a complete performance. Examples of performances that are complete include tying a shoe, reading a book, counting to 10, finishing a marathon, writing a letter, and solving a problem. A complete performance may be a competent one, such as counting to 10. More generally, however, we judge competent performances in terms of standards for the defining criteria. Finishing a marathon qualifies as a complete performance, but a competent performance may require finishing in a specified time.

Confidence is competence that is internalized. Confidence results from repeated recall of knowledge or successful application of skills in appropriate contexts. The confident individual feels assured that he or she can recall a skill (competence) or successfully complete a performance. Assessment that builds competence calls for affirmation of a performance, such as "That's right," or information that suggests change, such as "That's not quite correct; try this." Affirmation confirms complete performances and competent ones; recurring affirmation builds confidence. Because confidence is an internal state of being, students with the same level of competence often vary in their sense of confidence. In the classroom, student responses to questions or requests to complete a task vary in terms of their perceived capacity to do so. Thus, students offer responses ordered on a continuum from lack of any knowledge or skill such as "I don't know" through various levels of competence such as "I think it is . . . " or "It is . . ." and ultimately the confident "I know it is." When students recognize and internalize their competence in specific skills, they become confident in them. It is noteworthy that students can be confident not only in their knowledge or skill but in their lack of it. An important outcome of education is to recognize the difference between what you know and what you do not know.

A general sense of confidence is important for learning. Best characterized as belief in one's capacity to succeed, a general sense of confidence enables individuals to risk new learning and attempt new skills. General confidence also enhances students' capacity to seek and use assessment information. In the classroom environment, assessments that are informal, casual, and often unintended most often promote or diminish general confidence. Statements or attitudes toward students, such as perceptions of their abilities or aptitude, become powerful attributions that alter student confidence and subsequent performance. Comments or assessments that diminish students' general sense of confidence are indeed grave. Nourishing confidence is a highly valued outcome of schooling. But as teachers we have limited capacity to ensure confidence. We can be confident in students, but only the students can be confident in themselves.

Schooling historically dealt with competence in areas of basic literacy such as reading, writing, and arithmetic. As the curriculum became more diverse and complex, attention to competence gradually gave way to content coverage. Today, competence is difficult to attain, sometimes even difficult to define, given the breadth of curricular content, the pace of instruction, and assessment methods prevalently used. An assessment posture that helps students recognize their competence offers a useful framework for improving their performance.

Skills such as reading, writing, and numeracy are ones in which all students can become competent. These essential skills share attributes of being developmental and amenable to assessment given on an ongoing basis; providing assessment that effectively promotes them is crucial and forms the basis for subsequent discussion. I refer to this as assessment for learning; its focus is students, its message is constructive, and its primary messengers are teachers.

Assessment Principles

Assessment practices for learning derive from fundamental beliefs embodied in the 10 assessment principles described below. Assessment principles offered by others include those of Stiggins (1994), Linn and Gronlund (1995), and Wiggins (1993). The principles below, as well as those of others, should guide practice, not prescribe it. The principles offered here reflect beliefs about schooling, about students, and about learning. Beliefs play a major role in this book as well as a major role in assessment. It is important that each of us reflect on our experiences with assessment and adopt beliefs on which to build our assessment practices.

1. Instruction Touches the Mind; Assessment Touches the Heart

Assessments, formal or informal, considered or casual, intentional or not, powerfully affect people, particularly students. Learning thus includes both intellectual and emotional components. The assessment climate that students experience is a critical component of instruction and learning. Students' assessment experiences remain with them for a lifetime and substantially affect their capacity for future learning.

2. Assessment for Learning Is More a Process Than a Procedure

Assessment for learning is fundamentally a process, an attitude. Good assessment derives from genuine concern for individuals, often in a collective sense. Effective classroom assessment emphasizes learning, not testing; competence, not selection; instruction, not accountability. Classroom assessment practices can serve purposes other than learning, but only incidentally. The central issues regarding effective assessment are that students' performances be assessed fairly, accurately, purposefully, and sensitively. Assessment procedures such as tests or projects support the assessment process, but they are not the process.

3. The Teaching Profession Requires That Teachers Model Good Assessment Practice

Teachers who consider their practice a craft are in an excellent position to assume a professional posture and establish a classroom climate in which cooperative learning and collegial assessment lead to professional growth. Such a posture and climate can, as well, serve as a positive assessment example for students.

4. Classroom Assessment Is Primarily an Instructional Issue

Classroom assessment is *fundamentally* different from assessment used for selection and accountability. Tests designed for these purposes tend to be external to the classroom in intent, development, relevance, and use. The primary purpose of classroom assessment is to foster student learning and to promote student competence. Assessment practices designed for these purposes are an integral part of instruction. We need to once again associate assessment with instruction and learning. Good assessment practice is dependent on the purpose and nature of instructional goals. Assessment and instruction are inherently linked. Instructional purposes and goals should drive assessment instruments and procedures.

5. *Classroom Assessment Is Not Highly Technical*

Some would have educators believe that good assessment requires complex procedures and rigorous and expert development and is based on skills and concepts accessible to only a few. Some test purposes, practices, and contexts, especially those designed for selection decisions, do indeed call for highly technical skills. But most technical features of "tests" are neither practical nor necessary in routine assessment in the classroom. At the same time, providing fair, accurate, and consistent information to students is critical for all assessments.

6. *The Purpose of School Is to Help Students Become Competent in the Curriculum*

Most students come to school lacking competence in the curriculum. The process of becoming competent requires effective instruction and useful assessment information.

7. *A Positive Assessment Climate Combined With Effective Assessment Practices Encourages Students to Seek Assessment Information*

Effective instruction requires a positive assessment climate. The most productive learning environments are those in which students take an interest in and accept responsibility for their own learning. When this occurs, learners change from passive recipients of information to active participants in the learning process. For these *effective students,* mistakes take on meaning, success becomes associated with competence, and assessment becomes the means to an end rather than an end in itself.

8. *Creating Effective Assessment Practices Requires the Involvement of Teachers, Administrators, Students, Parents, and the Community*

Assessment practice affects not only those directly involved in instruction—students and school staff—but also parents and the community. Each group has a stake in the outcomes of instruction and assessment. Those who provide the day-to-day delivery of learning experiences need the support of colleagues, parents, administration, and the community.

9. *Assessment Is for Everyone*

No one escapes assessment; in particular, assessment is for everyone involved in education and is an essential part of the learning process. Educators and students benefit from effective assessment. Conditions that result in one-way assessment only diminish an important part of the learning climate. Thus, for example, constructive student assessment of teaching practices can improve instruction and learning. Effective professional assessment practices rely on teacher strengths, cooperative effort, and collegial feedback.

10. Everyone Has a Right to Good Assessment

Assessment is powerful. No one, be it student, administrator, or teacher, should have to endure poor assessment. In its more extreme forms, poor assessment practice constitutes abusive behavior. Classroom assessment should be positive in its impact on the individual and contain elements that make it challenging as well as useful. Fairness is essential.

The above set of principles is the basis for comments regarding assessment practice in this and subsequent chapters. Extension of these fundamental beliefs occurs throughout the book. In addition to these principles, it is necessary to recognize elements of the assessment experience that influence classroom assessment. Attention to these elements accompanies the beliefs that learning is as much an emotional act as an intellectual one and that assessment powerfully affects individuals.

Assessment Attributes

Classroom assessment as a critical component of learning plays a dominant role in the process of schooling. Classroom assessment has its own context, its own character, and its own climate. Effective classroom assessment requires attention to these factors and individual responses to it. Assessment is powerful. Because of its power, the delivery of assessment information requires our attention. Characteristics of assessments and their delivery influence the way others experience it. We enhance assessment practices by thoughtful attention to issues and attributes that characterize the assessment process itself. The assessment context and climate include attributes related to those who provide assessment information, those who receive assessment information, and the interplay between the two. Attention to these attributes illuminates student and teacher characteristics that impact learning and instruction.

The basis for the assessment attributes is the purpose of assessment; three common ones being selection, accountability, and learning. Assessments used for selection and accountability are similar in their impact on students, particularly in contrast to assessment for learning. A primary difference between assessments that serve accountability or selection decisions and those that serve learning is that the former address needs external to the student whereas the later serve the student directly. Irrespective of differences in purpose, individuals have the right to good assessment, whether it be of their performance or for selection or accountability. But this book is about assessment for learning—assessment fundamentally aligned with the purpose of schooling. As discussed here, the purpose of assessment is to guide the development of effective students and promote student competence. Consequently, assessment for learning demands attitudes and practices different from those used for selection and accountability.

Assessment practices portrayed in this book emphasize *students'* knowledge of their performance, *students'* awareness of competencies, and guided instruction regarding altering performances in ways necessary for building *students'* competence. There are substantial reasons for individuals other than students, including, of course, teachers, to know whether or not students can solve a problem, write a letter, read a map, and so forth. But it is imperative that *students* be afforded opportunity to build skills and a repertoire of knowledge that promote *their* sense of competence. One finds an example of this perspective in science outcome statements from *Benchmarks for Science Literacy* (National Science Foundation, 1994), in which outcome statements begin with "Students should know that . . . " From the assessment perspective taken here, emphasis should be on *students knowing.* Accenting the learners' point of view requires more attention to affirmation of student performance than in the past, whereas accountability to others can do with less attention. As detailed in later chapters, increased affirmation of student performances requires that learning goals be identified and described in ways that clearly identify to the learner what needs to be done and that successful completion culminates in skills, attitudes, or behaviors that students can recognize and experience. Affirming students' skills, attitudes, and behaviors is an important assessment function. Affirmation is what turns a performance into an accomplishment. Affirmations are a common part of skill building during the early years, as when a child successfully ties his or her shoes. Affirmation of competence appears to steadily diminish as students progress through their schooling, giving way to more quantitative measures such as percentage correct and grade point average.

Assessment information is effective as received, not as given. Consequently, the nature of information given and its presentation affect its usefulness for others. Assessment is a constant companion of instruction to promote learning. The way students experience assessment has a lot to do with their capacity to use it. Considering attributes that characterize assessment information and the assessment process helps us think about it from the recipient's perspective. Attributes spanning six areas accompany assessment practices to promote learning: authority, the kind of assessment sought, the nature of assessment information, its timeliness, the emotional charge attached to assessment information, and the climate or setting in which assessment takes place. These assessment attributes, taken together, serve as powerful components of teacher-student interactions. From the professional teacher's perspective, they are critical to establishing assessment practices that enhance learning.

Authority

The first of six assessment attributes is authority. When speaking of authority in the assessment context, a useful synonym might be *expert.* In this sense, students experience an authority-based classroom environment when knowledge appears to reside in the expert teacher. In an authority-based classroom, students may even believe that teachers are responsible for the subject itself. Thus, students may miss the inherent logic and structure of geometry and instead focus their energy on course requirements dictated by the teacher. Apprehension replaces comprehension and students seek a passing score in place of competence.

Students come to experience and recognize authority in a variety of ways. For example, over the course of school, students from kindergarten through graduate school have many opportunities to both complete written work and respond to their teachers' written instructions. Teachers occasionally judge students' writing as unclear or unintelligible. The familiar teacher comment is that students should rewrite a paper to make it more intelligible. Similarly, students may occasionally experience difficulty comprehending written directions provided by teachers. When students relate that directions are not clear, teachers direct them to re-read the directions or to read them more carefully.

Some assessment practices contribute to the difficulty students experience in dissociating learning and authority; one such practice is the pervasive aura of mystery that surrounds testing environments. Test content, test format, and performance criteria, left unspecified, speak to who decides what is important, who is in charge, and who defines competence. Students who seek competence need information and direction. It is difficult for students to attain competence that is not defined. Stiggins (1994) repeatedly emphasizes the importance of clear assessment targets and he devotes and entire chapter to them (pp. 59-80). Wiggins (1993), addressing test security, asks, "Why would we take for granted that students do not have a right to full knowledge and justification of the form and content of each test and the standards by which their work will be judged?" (p. 73).

Authority also impacts teacher-student relationships in significant ways. Knowledge perceived as residing in the teacher and assessment information channeled through the teacher result in students and teachers finding themselves in opposition to one another. When this occurs, it becomes the student's job to ferret out information teachers consider important, to outwit them, to seek their permission, to follow their prescribed style, and to find out what will be on the test. Gullickson (1993) discusses this issue in terms of teachers becoming the "gatekeeper[s] of information important to the individual student's learning" (p. 22). By way of contrast, viewing knowledge as independent of the instructional leader and sharing assessment information with students allow teachers to become a guiding resource who help students gain knowledge, understanding, and skills. In such settings, students, emancipated from control by and reaction to authority, become free to seek assessment. This characteristic—seeking assessment of performance—characterizes both effective students and professional educators.

Kind of Assessment Sought

The kind of assessment sought reflects individual student characteristics, such as their assessment history, the assessment purpose (information vs. affirmation), and the relationship between the assessor and the individual assessed. Assessment information may be avoided, unsolicited, or sought. Students come to school with unique assessment histories that affect their openness to assessment information. Depending in part on individual histories, students may seek some kinds of information and avoid others. Students who seek assessment of their performances have an advantage over those who do not. Helping students develop the capacity to seek and use assessment information contributes to their becoming effective students. Assessment practices, including the assessment climate, contribute to the willingness of students to seek assessment.

Teachers recognize varied assessment situations and appreciate the difference between the politics of assessment and the assessment itself. The distinction between formative and summative assessment define some of these differences; others are due to personal and political aspects of assessment. As an illustration of the purpose and politics of assessment, consider the kind of assessment information sought by someone preparing to deliver a speech compared with assessment sought by someone preparing a speech to deliver. Critique, suggestions, and discussion may all be helpful to someone preparing a talk, but such assessment is of little value to someone about to approach the podium. Students, too, need information and affirmation as they pursue competence. Information helps students become competent; affirmation helps them know when they are.

In some instances, affirmation is appropriately given for performances that do not meet competence standards. It is helpful for students to receive affirmation of a complete performance, such as an initial draft of an essay. Affirmation in this instance lets the student know that she or he understands what the performance is and provides encouragement to proceed.

Nature and Amount of Information

Assessment information varies in what it conveys to the recipient. The nature of assessment information can relate a simple summary score, such as percentage correct or a letter grade; indicate answers that are right and wrong; or provide descriptive statements, such as comments on a writing assignment that offer specific information regarding areas related to writing or the content of the assignment. Information may also vary according to whether it is based on known facts, such as that the earth is about 24,000 miles in circumference, or on opinions or preferences, such as a preferred writing style. Students, particularly young ones, may find it difficult to differentiate between assessment based on a teacher's opinion or "objective" facts.

The amount of assessment information also varies considerably, from no information at all to copious comments and corrections. From a learning standpoint, minimal information limits students opportunities to address limitations in their work. On the other hand, an avalanche of assessment information, especially with limited time to respond, can overwhelm students. In short, the nature of assessment information is critical not only in terms of its accuracy but in terms of its impact on the recipient of the information.

Timeliness and Time to Use Assessment Information

The timeliness of assessment information and the opportunity to use it constructively affect its value. When, for example, the pace of instruction limits or prohibits students' opportunities to learn from their mistakes or to affirm their competence, students lose a learning opportunity and teachers waste time and energy providing the information. Scoring papers is a laborious and time-consuming process. When this energy produces only summary indicators of student performance used for record keeping and grading exclusively, students are shortchanged.

Emotional Charge

Emotional charge is part of the character of assessment information. The emotional charge associated with assessment information impacts individuals through characteristics such as volume, inflection, tone, and word choice. It can be communicated in writing as well as verbally. Like the kind of information sought, the emotional charge produces unique reactions that depend on individuals' assessment history. Some students, for example, freeze when spoken to in a loud voice. The emotional charge of assessment information is relevant for both the assessor and the person being assessed. In the person assessed, it might range from hurt—"You didn't like my paper"—to exhilaration—"I finally got it!" In the assessor, it might reflect anger or fear—"Don't ever play in the street again"—or pride—"You did great!" Thoughtful application of emotionally charged assessment information can be productive, but its potential for a negative impact on students must be recognized.

Assessment Setting

The assessment setting refers to the general context or climate in which assessment information is exchanged. Setting characteristics include factors such as whether the instructional climate is cooperative or competitive and what method is used to distribute assessment information. Assessment information can reward or punish or provide suggestions for improvement. Discussions about a community of learners often reflect this attribute.

Individual competence and the power assessment has to impact people are connected by the belief that learning is as much an emotional act as an intellectual one. Learning is an emotional experience because individuals strive to be competent and assessment information provides evidence of whether or not they are. Learning thus involves personal risk. The implication is that classroom assessment practices should afford students opportunities to risk learning with some measure of safety.

These assessment attributes along with the principles described earlier are the bases for assessment practices detailed in this book; they are not, however, prescriptive. Education is a local community enterprise and instruction and assessment are the responsibility of professional teachers. Teaching is a challenging profession, one that demands multiple skills, including assessment. Although many assessment procedures serve external requirements, teachers are in a position to address the needs of students. Effective assessment practices for learning begin with thoughtful consideration by teachers, individually and collectively. Ongoing development occurs in the context of their use by those who use them. The recommended review process permits local and individual determination of assessment procedures and practices.

An Assessment Review Process

Teaching methods and assessment practices in education often circumvent careful examination of foundational beliefs and principles by the professionals who use them. Assessment procedures in particular seem to take place in a hand-me-down fashion. Training in assessment has been absent or is not relevant to assessment for learning. As professional educators, we need to look beneath and beyond our assessment practices. Beneath our practices lie the beliefs we hold, the assumptions we make, and the reality of things we cannot change. Beyond our practices is the impact they have on students. Effective programs, effective practices, and effective change by professionals require their commitment and beliefs.

Stated or not, day-to-day educational practices reflect particular perspectives, foundational beliefs, and assumptions. Educators are sometimes encouraged or directed to alter their practices to conform to some instructional model that includes instructional formats and sequences and prescribed student activities. Textbook objectives, end-of-chapter quizzes, and other (often helpful) instructional aids are common examples. These instructional components and procedures prescribe what teachers do and subsequently impact what students learn. But unexamined and perfunctory use of ready-made instructional tools leaves professionals without a sufficient framework to create or modify practices to suit their needs. "New" assessment practices easily fall into this category. Shifting to alternative methods of assessing students without first considering assessment beliefs and goals

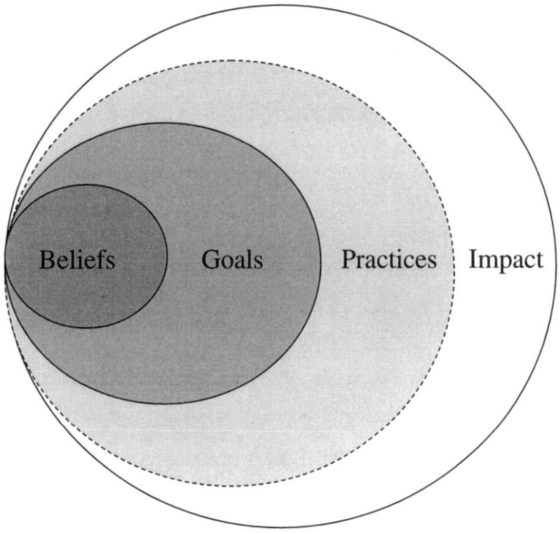

Figure 1.1. Four-Level Review Process

leaves educators without a sound basis for evaluating the impact of their assessment practices. This in turn limits effective application of alternative and current assessment practices and leads to confusion on the part of staff, students, parents, and the community.

A simple four-level review process serves as a framework for examining assessment practice (see Figure 1.1). At the core of the review process are assessment beliefs, assumptions, and constraints that serve to fix assessment and instructional goals. Practices address the stated goals. Finally, monitoring the impact of practices becomes the focus for evaluating and changing them if necessary.

At the core of practice are beliefs, assumptions, and facts. Ideas defined at this basic level become the bases for professional activities. A variety of beliefs and assumptions are at hand, such as that everyone has a right to good assessment, all students can learn, students seek personal competence, and the purpose of school is to promote competence and confidence. Facts such as external conditions also affect goal setting and thus impact and sometimes constrain assessment goals and practices. For example, irrespective of one's beliefs about testing, state statutes may require that standardized tests be given to all students at certain grade levels.

At the second review level, beliefs, assumptions, and facts are transformed into assessment goals. Assessment goals might be to promote competence in reading, to have students perform well on a national examination, or to establish an assessment climate that promotes learning. A personal professional goal might be to examine and consider a new approach to assessment of reading comprehension.

The third level, practices, includes those procedures, processes, and methods that serve to achieve stated goals, including the selection and appropriate use of assessment procedures. Practices assume special importance, since they, rather than beliefs or goals, directly impact students. It is at the point of impact that assessment becomes meaningful, useful, harmful, or irrelevant. As noted earlier, assessment information is effective as received, not as delivered. The impact assessment information has on students is what matters. The final and indispensable step in this review process is to ascertain the value assessments have for students. How they react to and use information is the critical criterion for effective assessment practices.

Beliefs and goals become criteria on which to judge practice. So, for example, we might endorse the *belief* that the purpose of assessment is to promote competence. An attendant goal might be to review and develop assessment practices that help students recognize their competence or that provide information necessary to build competence in developing areas. Simply providing students with summary scores, such as percentage correct, means that our practice is at odds with stated assessment beliefs and goals.

The process described here is only a general guide for assessment review by individuals or groups. Individual reviews are valued because assessment has critical implications for learning and because teachers manage their own assessment practices. Notions relating assessment practices and professional growth presented in Chapter 5 suggest that individual teachers benefit substantially from discussions with colleagues, however. Regardless of the specific procedure, this reflective process illuminates connections among assessment beliefs, goals, practices, and their impact on students; meaningful change in assessment practice requires more than shifting to portfolios or performance assessments.

Author's Note

The assessment principles and attributes offered in this initial chapter provide a foundation for remaining discussion as well as a perspective to consider in the review of assessment practice. "New" assessments, authentic assessments, performance assessments, and portfolios are attempts to connect assessment practice to a more traditional view of learning, to return to assessment practices that promote student learning and competence. As you proceed, remember that your review may lead you to maintain your current assessment practices or to change them. Irrespective of the outcome, you need to begin your review by stating, shaping, and adopting assessment beliefs and principles to build or maintain effective assessment practices.

As you continue through this book, please keep in mind that the ideas suggested here follow from beliefs embedded or explicit in this and subsequent chapters. Although this book emphasizes classroom assessment practice, the goal is to restore student learning in terms of competence and confidence, often discussed in terms of application, synthesis, and evaluation. I hope your review of instruction and assessment will take you beyond the guise of content coverage, factual information, and operational definitions to more meaningful educational experiences for your students. As you consider assessment, rely on your beliefs, value your experiences, and main-

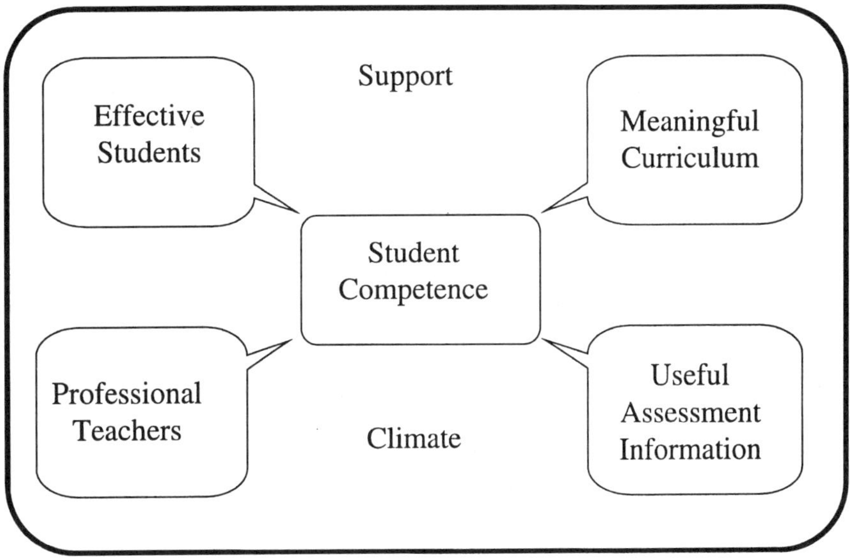

Figure 1.2. Effective Learning Elements

tain confidence in your effective practices. I hope you will find that the ideas presented represent basic and rather obvious notions about instruction and assessment that make sense to you for promoting student learning. To that end, I encourage you to reflect on your own personal assessment experiences both as a professional educator and as a student, to imagine how assessment practice might impact others and how it might be improved, and to consider student and professional competence in terms of high-quality work.

The ideas presented in this and succeeding chapters represent a perspective about assessment practices in terms of the beliefs on which they are founded and the goals to which they aspire. These ideas are not prescriptive in intent. Please *consider* the ideas presented here, *consider* their implications for assessment practice, and *consider* changing your practice to reflect this perspective. Consideration of these ideas offers you opportunity to examine *your* beliefs, goals, and practices regarding assessment and their impact on your students. The process of doing so will benefit you personally and professionally and will likely add to the value and meaning of this book for you.

The ideas in this book follow from the fundamental belief that the purpose of schooling is to promote student competence in the curriculum. The interdependent elements needed to achieve this purpose include effective students, a meaningful curriculum, useful assessment information, a professional staff posture, and a supportive work environment. The next several chapters address these essential and interdependent components (see Figure 1.2). Connections among them suggest that effective schools are those where effective students pursue competence in a meaningful curriculum that becomes known to them through useful instruction and assessment practices orchestrated by professional educators.

The next chapter suggests that effective students, in particular students who seek and use assessment information, are indispensable for effective schools. The third chapter reminds us that a meaningful curriculum along with effective instruction and assessment lead to high-quality work. Chapter 4 extends the discussion of assessment practices in terms of information use. A major point there is that the main criterion for choosing appropriate assessment procedures is assessment purpose. Chapter 5 examines the nature of assessment for the professional educator. Assessment practices and criteria that produce effective students apply to the *professional* educator; this suggests that good assessment is as critical for educators as it is for students. Finally, Chapter 6 addresses the crucial issue of the support needed to help educators review their instruction and assessment practices.

This book is also about courage and commitment. It seeks to outline conditions and practices by which students can pursue competence through meaningful instruction and useful assessment information. It seeks to expand professional skills in assessment through assessment. For some educators, courage will be needed to give others permission to explore assessment options and grant them authority to change their practice; for other educators, courage will be needed to implement assessment options and share in the responsibility for changing practice. In both instances, commitment to professional practice and student learning are essential.

2

Developing Effective Students

“We need to develop in students the expectation to succeed and the capacity to learn from assessment information.”

The initial chapter began the discussion of assessment with general principles and dimensions that guide assessment for learning. Assessment is an essential duty of teachers. As will be seen, assessment not only is important for student learning but plays a major role in professional growth as well. The key attribute of effective students and effective teachers is the aspiration to develop personal competence. For educators, this means competence in their professional duties; for students it means competence in instructional areas, such as reading, writing, the arts, and so forth. This parallel to professionalism means that positive assessment attitudes, effective assessment skills, and a favorable assessment climate are important for teachers and students alike. Here, the focus for discussion is developing students for whom mistakes take on meaning, success becomes associated with competence, and assessment becomes the means to the end rather than an end in itself.

Over the years, an assessment (or testing) system emerged in which the primary purposes became selection and accountability (grades, student grouping, and class rank). The shift in emphasis from performance to selection and grades that evolved over the past 50 years has diminished the sense of competence and confidence that students carry away from their school experience. Indeed, current testing and grading practices often ignore students' competence and may actually erode their sense of confidence. Grades or scores may or may not adequately reflect competent performance, but they clearly do not emphasize performance and learning. Testing for selection, placement, and accountability constrains learning of important skills and limits the time to affirm what students know; such constraints can adversely affect students' belief in their capacity to perform, their sense of understanding material, and their inclination for future learning. This book, particularly this chapter, is about assessment in which the primary purpose is to nourish students' learning, develop their competence, and build their confidence.

In simpler times, assessment addressed personal competence—competence defined by practical skills that family members passed on to their children. Young adults learned useful skills such as carpentry, farming, or food preparation at the knee of their father or mother. In some regions and cultures, this practice continues. In more recent times, however, particularly over the past 75 years, many adults left the home for work and no longer passed on vocational skills to their children. Public schools began to fill the educational void caused by this exodus, and instruction focused on basic literacy skills. The purpose of assessment practices in these early schools was simply to help students develop basic competence in skills such as reading, writing, and arithmetic.

As knowledge expanded, as the need for skilled labor increased, and as competition for college entrance and good jobs became more intense and widespread, the nature of assessment changed from emphasizing competence to emphasizing selection, accountability, and efficiency. These emphases, along with rapidly expanding content, ushered in a shift to curriculum outcomes stated in objective terms and easily measured. At about the same time, interest grew in predicting who should enter and who might best succeed in trade schools and colleges. This interest in prediction spawned large-scale testing efforts designed to provide evidence regarding achievement or aptitude that would identify students most worthy of filling limited classes in universities and trade schools. Thus, testing became associated with standardized tests that relied on efficient multiple-choice questions and machine-scored formats. As this testing emphasis advanced and the amount of content expanded, attention to assessment of student performance diminished. Tests increasingly became proxies for performance with their use directed at predicting future school success rather than performance.

Following the lead of national testing programs, schools increasingly came to rely on multiple-choice and short answer formats to provide assessment information. The content of these tests emphasized knowledge and facts (although not exclusively), as opposed to the more complex skills of synthesis, analysis, and evaluation. Quantitative values, especially percentage correct, easily and defensibly derived, became the basis for computing numeric grades. Results of these assessments were used for selection and placement decisions such as such as tracking, for determining grade point averages, and for establishing class rank.

In brief, assessment practices currently found in our schools have been heavily influenced by expanding knowledge and attendant interest in broad content coverage, competition for limited postsecondary opportunities, selection and placement decisions, and efficient scoring procedures. One outcome of these emphases has been that student and parent interest in academic progress has become based more on comparison than performance; concern with instructional assessment has increasingly become tied to selection and placement decisions resulting from tests rather than providing a basis for instruction and learning.

In very recent times, there have been increasing calls for changing the way we educate students—for developing students who can write better, think better, learn better, and adapt better. Concurrently, there have been increasing calls for changing the way we assess students' work. There is a growing sense that assessment practices currently used in our schools are inadequate. One proposed solution is to replace existing tests with "new" ones such as portfolios, performance assessments, and "authentic" assessment. Increasingly, these methods are being tried by local school districts.

A major point of this book is that assessment is a powerful force that affects students in substantial and important ways. Review of the beliefs, assessment goals, and criteria used to judge the value of assessment strategies and the reasons for implementing alternative strategies is important. Simply changing from one assessment format to another, without thoughtful consideration of their use and implications for students, is unlikely to result in more effective practices.

Improving assessment practice requires examining the impact that assessment beliefs, assessment goals, and attendant assessment practices have on individual students. It should be obvious that new assessment strategies and procedures must be those that best help students become more effective learners. Assessment practices not only alter what students learn in the short term, but they also affect students' sense of personal competence and shape their future opportunity and capacity for learning. Many students experience assessment as personal failure. For some students, failure is receiving a grade of B+ instead of an A. For other students, continuous negative assessment experiences cause them to drop out of school. The personal and long-lasting impact of assessment practices on students warrants thoughtful review of these practices.

Review of assessment practices requires that we determine what student characteristics and qualities regarding assessment and learning we want to promote to help students become effective and then examine current assessment practices in light of these desired characteristics and qualities. If current practices do not achieve stated goals for students, then we need to change assessment experiences, including the assessment climate. Changing assessment practices includes review of alternative assessment strategies and procedures. As this chapter progresses, an emphasis is that student readiness for assessment and experience with it directly impact their learning, now and in the future. In addition, student readiness for assessment can be identified and capabilities developed that improve their effectiveness as learners.

The remainder of this chapter examines assessment practice and its impact on students. In the next several sections, characteristics that describe effective students, especially in terms of their using assessment information, are explored.

Characteristics of Assessment-Ready Students

Assessment readiness means much more than simply test wiseness or knowledge of study strategies that optimize chances to get a high test score. This is not to say that these are not important skills; when assessment is an add-on to instruction or when it is external to the instructional setting, the assessment method and format likely affect performance. Preparing students to deal with these external assessments is in their best interests. But the perspective here is that effective students are those who can readily *use* assessment information to build competence. Assessment-ready students possess four characteristics essential to enable them to use assessment information effectively. The assessment-ready student is one who

- Seeks personal competence and confidence
- Possesses both the expectation to succeed and the capacity to fail
- Views assessment as a means to an end rather than an end in itself
- Recognizes high-quality work and its relation to personal competence

Competence and Confidence

Seeking personal competence is an integral part of ordinary human development. Children begin seeking competence at an early age. Beginning with their first steps and first words, children continue to seek competence and independence in tying their shoes, recognizing letters, naming colors, counting to 10, or reading a book. Children experience such performances holistically, and parents, peers, siblings, or teachers affirm them holistically; each is a complete performance. "Mastering" these tasks contributes to the child's successful struggle for independence and control; the performance is personally satisfying. Although mastery means many things and has many levels, the fundamental characteristic necessary for competence is the successful completion of a task or performance.

The pursuit and maintenance of competence, present during the early childhood years, continue in the formative years and adult life, first during school and later in work. Neither acquiring nor maintaining competence is ever fully ensured. Regardless of age, new tasks and new skills are challenges, some more challenging than others. Nevertheless, the criterion remains the same: A competent performance requires that there be a sense of completeness. Tying a shoe requires more than tying the first part of the knot; reading a book for comprehension requires more than reading words. A competent performance is experienced as one that is complete and effective. It is not, however, necessarily a perfect performance; nor does its success depend on the performance of others.

A competent performance is independent of the performance of others. This is of some consequence for education, as it implies that all students can be successful. As was stated earlier, the defining attribute of competence is completing a defined task; so, for example, a competence could be reading a book. Any student who "reads" a complete book experiences that competency. It is a complete task. Reading a book in 2 hours may represent a perfectly adequate performance, even if most people can read the same book in half that time. This simple example illustrates a fundamental limitation for assessments that are comparison based, namely, that they often rely on performance dimensions, such as time, that either go beyond competence or that skirt the competence issue altogether.

Assessment is a key component for developing competence. To become competent requires comments or responses that inform the individual of progress toward the performance goal. The culminating assessment, either by personal observation (self-assessment) or the critique of another person (teacher), is that the performance has met some adequate level or standard. This standard may be set at any point that includes a complete performance, the initial requisite characteristic of competence.

Confidence, related to a specific skill or performance, is a step beyond competence. Confidence results from the successful and repeated application of a specific competence. As described in Chapter 1, one cannot become truly confident at a task until one has done it. Students gain confidence in their capacity to read by reading or in counting to 10 by doing so. Repeated and successful application of skills lead to confidence. Confidence is only attained after successful performances such as reading or counting. The common phrase, "Experience is the best teacher," implies that learning involves doing.

The Expectation to Succeed and the Capacity to Fail

Closely related to developing confidence is the idea that assessment-ready students expect to be successful in achieving a learning outcome. But if these same students fail, they are neither devastated nor daunted in their pursuit of a particular performance; effective students expect to succeed on the next attempt or the one thereafter. Lacking these qualities, students come to believe they cannot learn and, fearing failure, risk nothing or try nothing.

It is important to distinguish between general confidence, the expectation to succeed, and the confidence one achieves as a result of affirmation of performance or application of competence. A general sense of confidence helps students attempt learning, whereas specific confidence results from successful experiences or applications of competencies. Nothing promotes success like success. A general sense of confidence, including the capacity to attempt new learnings, is an essential attribute of effective students. Confident students approach learning tasks with the expectation of being successful. The general sense of confidence discussed here precedes confidence resulting from successful application of a specific competence.

The second of this complementary pair of assessment attributes is the capacity to fail. In our culture, as in many others, failure carries with it severe negative connotations; no one wants to fail. The fear of failure often dictates what individuals are willing to attempt. Yet, achieving competence at challenging and useful tasks nearly always requires multiple attempts, frequent failures, and perseverance. Assessment practices that encourage students to review and revise their work reward perseverance and allow them to turn "failure" into success. An important attribute of effective instruction and assessment is that it helps students see progress toward goals even when full attainment is not realized.

Assessment as a Means to an End Rather Than an End in Itself

Many students experience classroom assessment as a grade based on results from formal written tests and quizzes; written assignments completed in class or at home; and, sometimes, tardiness, late papers, and behavior. In most cases, results are lasting and immutable, or at least appear to be so, in the sense that they contribute to a permanent record. This assessment philosophy sends the message that assessment, usually in the form of a grade, is terminal. Tests signal the end of an instructional unit and signify the merit associated with work completed to that point.

Assessment neither viewed as a test nor tied to a grade becomes an opportunity to facilitate learning and build competence. This perspective on assessment includes what I call a recovery performance, that is, a performance achieved after one or more unsuccessful attempts. Instances when students succeed after failure, particularly after multiple failures, are perhaps the most powerful of all learning experiences, experiences that establish confidence in one's capacity for future learning. As these instances occur, students develop expectant persistence, the capacity to persevere until they achieve the desired outcome. Assessment that is ongoing and continuous enhances expectant persistence.

Assessment, given on an ongoing basis and experienced as information tied to instruction and performance, enables students to use assessment. Cast in this light, assessment becomes a way to build not only knowledge, skills, and competence but also a sense of confidence; it is this sense that contributes to students' recognition of their capacity for further learning. Appropriate use of assessment that acknowledges completed performances (affirmation) provides powerful reinforcement necessary for developing effective students. Even close approximations to complete performance are sometimes deserving of a "Yes!" or "You've nearly got it."

Viewing assessment as part of instruction rather then the end of instruction necessitates it be provided on an ongoing basis. Commonly, instruction ends with assessment (a test). When results of those assessments connote failure, it not only leaves students with a sense of defeat but communicates either that the performance is not important or that students are not competent in an area that is important. This does not necessarily imply that students who do well on a test believe themselves to be competent; their perception may be that even though they tested well, they lack sufficient understanding of the material to apply the information in a useful way. Understanding material at a competent level requires application or synthesis, normally developed through progressive and continuous instruction, practice, and assessment. This process is particularly critical for important knowledge and skills that warrant high-quality work.

Recognizing High-Quality Work

Students come to know that learning tasks are important when teachers review and reteach them. If the task is important, teachers ask twice. Significant learning tasks receive ongoing instruction and continuous assessment, stress quality of performance, and reward improvement. The common essay, for example, provides opportunities for reviewing writing skills and giving helpful comments and suggestions. The assessment process thus portrays writing as an important skill, one that merits a high degree of quality.

Not all learning necessarily involves the same level of quality. There are at least three ways that quality can vary—by developmental level (grade), by importance (survey or exploratory courses), and by student choice. Elements of work quality that vary by grade level include obvious differences in criteria or standards for the 5th-grade students versus those used for the 12th-grade students. But students might also choose a quality level, as long as the essential notion of developing competence remains. Some may argue that student choice regarding quality only invites "minimum competence." Justification for varied quality, irrespective of its source, requires defining competence, beginning with a complete performance that is developmentally appropriate and in line with the curriculum. Instructional standards that address minimum competence need to emphasize *competence* rather than minimum standards and complete performances rather than percentage correct. If students are to become competent, they need information; if students are to become confident, they need affirmation. If students are to seek assessment as a means to an end, then instruction needs to focus on performance, and if high-quality performance is a goal, it requires ongoing and continuous assessment for a reasonable number of important outcomes.

Review of Assessment Practice

If the four characteristics of effective students described above—seeking personal competence, having the expectation to succeed and capacity to fail, viewing assessment as a means to an end rather than as an end in itself, and recognizing high-quality work—are judged desirable for students to respond to assessment information in a meaningful and effective way, then one criterion for reviewing assessment practices is whether they promote these characteristics in students. What follows is an overview of instructional and assessment practices that affect students' effectiveness as learners and their capacity to seek and use assessment information. Taken together, these instructional practices and conditions make up the assessment environment in which students operate and constitute their assessment experience. Although not intended as a comprehensive review of assessment practice, the comments below suggest areas that deserve attention for developing effective students.

Belief in Students

Perhaps the single most important student attribute that helps students seek assessment is having the confidence and courage to take educational risks. Students need to acquire the expectation of succeeding and the capacity to use assessment information constructively. Teachers who communicate belief in students' capacity for learning enhance their confidence and courage. Most disheartening to see in classrooms are students who have come to believe they cannot learn; such students have lost the expectation that they can succeed. Particularly troublesome is the commonly heard phrase that a student or students just do not have the ability to do the required work or meet the desired standards. Where this perception exists, even privately, students come to believe that they lack the wherewithal to learn. Sometimes, this perception exists because a student is of one gender or the other, belongs to a particular ethnic group, dresses in a certain way, comes from a nonstandard family structure, or behaves in a particular way. From an instructional perspective, it is well to remember that performance is more "want to" than can. Multiple motivational factors affect performance, including fundamental beliefs or attitudes toward learners, such as about their ability; this is especially true of attitudes held by teachers. Expressed belief in students communicated by others is a potent force, especially for instilling in students confidence in their capacity to learn.

Taking educational risks requires a certain amount of confidence that one has at least a reasonable chance for success. Building students' confidence is important because it allows them to attempt new skills and enables them to accept and benefit from assessment information. Student confidence is a crucial matter because risk is part of the learning environment. Perhaps as much of education deals with the issue of confidence as with the mechanics of learning. Assessment plays a dominant role in helping students become confident as learners; positive experiences with assessment are important, particularly during the first years of schooling.

One way to build confidence is through affirmation; yet, affirming student performance is a frequently neglected assessment practice. Knowledge or skills (competence) in themselves do not instill confidence; rather confidence results from personal affirmation or from successful application of knowledge. Confidence is especially critical for the most important educational goals and objectives. Assessment practices based on a model of teach, test, and move on rarely lead to competence and almost never contribute to confidence. Students need affirmation, especially for learnings deemed most important, such as reading skills, writing skills, thinking skills, and math skills. Students benefit from responses that affirm their performances; affirmation is what turns a performance into an accomplishment.

Promoting High-Quality Work

As suggested earlier in this chapter, another characteristic of effective students is a sense of quality and its relationship to personal competence. Seeking assessment implies a desire to improve a performance to the point of achieving competence (at some acceptable level). High-quality performance is something that students can come to recognize; they may not always achieve it and they may not always attempt to achieve it, but they can, for the most part, recognize it when they see it. In a real sense, students benefit from the belief that high quality is within their grasp, even if they choose not to pursue it. From an effective student's perspective, pursuit of high quality is as important as achieving it. Students may gain more from pursuing and achieving high quality in one area or on one project than from feigning or ignoring high quality in all their work. The sense of control that students gain from choosing whether they will aspire to high-quality work can help preserve their sense of confidence for future learning. Of course, students need to be aware of the consequences that attend consistent lack of quality. At the same time, teachers need to be aware of the demands placed on students and determine just how much quality they can reasonably produce. Thus, the pace and content of instruction have important implications for the quality of work.

Connections among the pace of instruction, broad content coverage, assessment format, and grades based on a percentage correct model are commonplace. Demands associated with a fast instructional pace lead to loss of spontaneity and diminished opportunities to affirm student competence. An instructional pace that does not provide sufficient time for review and revision of performance and does not lend itself to students' occasional need to play with ideas or create their own knowledge structures does not encourage high-quality work. A fast instructional pace frequently accompanies the learning of ready-made structures and facts. Attendant assessment activities may be chosen based on scoring efficiency and rely almost exclusively on factual content using multiple-choice or short answer formats. Although such formats are appropriate for some curricular elements, they may be limited for others.

Finally, discussions about the quality of work should acknowledge that not all students fit the same mold. Permitting student participation in educational decisions encourages them to take personal responsibility for their work and allows them to follow their personal interests. Some students might reasonably study areas with minimal interest; such areas may be more palatable and more aggressively pursued when promoted more as options than requirements. Furthermore, aspirations toward associate degrees, trades, community colleges, apprenticeships, business, or any other pursuit constitute choice, not failure. If one outcome of education is to preserve choice and opportunity, we need to consider assessment strategies that promote individual choice.

Criteria and Standards

Establishing performance criteria and setting performance standards, topics much debated in education, are complex issues. Criteria and standards affect both students and teachers. Criteria refer to the elements used to describe or define performances such as time, punctuation, accuracy, or memorization. Standards here refer to performance specifications that students and teachers agree on to describe competent performances according to the identified criteria. So, for example, when time is a criterion used with addition problems, the amount of time allotted to complete a given set of problems becomes a standard. Other definitions of standards and statements about standards often refer to content coverage. For example, a frequent recommendation is to set standards high but attainable, and in some cases higher standards lead to raising graduation requirements. But when raising standards simply translates into more content, more courses, and a faster pace, the result may run counter to desired instructional goals, such as doing high-quality work. From a student's point of view, standards that emphasize broad content and a fast pace make producing high-quality work and gaining competence difficult. Conversely, when the student goal is competence, high-quality work is described and encouraged. As a matter of practice, therefore, it may prove more effective to affirm students' pursuit of high-quality work rather than to demand it.

Criteria and standards affect students' efforts in the near and long term. In particular, demands associated with fixed criteria and standards can be exasperating for many students. Student effort can vary from no effort at all to personal best. It is reasonable that schools demand students make a minimal effort to engage in the learning process. Beyond a minimal effort is the opportunity for students to contribute a substantial effort or their personal best. Personal best can be encouraged but not demanded. Performances can be ordered using criteria and standards that begin with a complete performance, continue through various levels of competence, and finally attain perfection. Developing and maintaining effective students requires that student effort relate to competence, beginning with a complete performance.

Three standards levels are complete performances, competent performances, and competitive performances. Performances are complete when they address the criteria in some minimal way. Competent performances meet specified standards. For example, the criterion of accuracy might carry a standard of 80% correct. Finally, competitive standards (may) include added criteria (e.g., speed), standards that exceed those signifying competence (e.g., 98%

vs. 80% accuracy), or added content in terms of depth or breadth. Connections between student effort and performance standards are as follows:

TABLE 2.1 Connections Between Effort and Performance Standards

Levels of Student Effort	*Performance Standards*
Personal best	Competitive standard
Effort toward a competent performance	Competence standard
Effort toward a complete performance	Complete performance
Minimal or no effort	Incomplete or not attempted

The relationship between student effort and performance standards is less than perfect. But it is helpful if students come to recognize connections between effort and performance, although this can be difficult for them to do if they are faced with singular standards. Standards, as expectations, can disallow students opportunity to experience the personal rewards that attend personal best efforts. Therefore, we need to appreciate students' efforts and affirm their progress as well as their competence. Affirmation of performance means it addresses specified criteria or meets some standard. We describe performances relative to a performance goal; affirmation signifies that the goal is achieved; information suggests more (and what) needs to be done to achieve the goal.

From an individual student perspective, a personal best effort represents the competitive standard. It is important, then, that we appreciate students' effort, the work they produce and their seeking and using assessment information to improve their performance. Assessment information addresses students' performances and affirms their competence or progress toward it. Students' best performances validate their competence. Students experience competence through completed tasks; sometimes—perhaps often—they do not attempt them. Effective students may choose to preserve their personal best efforts for particular subjects, topics, or interests; doing so does not make for a "bad" student.

Giving and receiving assessment information is instructionally valid independent of grades. For example, students benefit from grammar or spelling information even when a writing performance emphasizes argumentation as the primary performance criterion. We need to remember, however, that assessment information is most valued when it helps build individual skills. Simply making changes in essays based on teacher comments or peer review, for example, may lead to a "better" paper, but not improved writing competence. Collaborative performances along with skills to work collaboratively are valuable, but independence and competence are primary individual goals for schooling.

Setting standards is problematic, but without them students struggle for direction. Criteria and standards containing information students and teachers agree on that describe competent performances help students "get the picture"—help them *see* performance elements; assessment information, along with content specification, helps students know when they are done. They can still add to their competence through extended learnings, additional criteria, or competitive standards. Stiggins (1994) describes performance definition as "achievement targets." In other words, assessment directed at student competence emphasizes criteria and performance standards in place of competitive ones. Criteria may be thought of as qualitative standards. The preference for qualitative standards arises from competence being defined as a complete performance, such as walking, tying a shoe, writing a letter, or understanding a concept. For example, a qualitative standard associated with multiplication could be that the students connect it with addition. A student who grasps this meaning can do multiplication—that is understands multiplication. In contrast, demonstrating knowledge of multiplication by correctly answering at least 90 out of 100 problems in 10 minutes represents a quantitative performance standard that may demonstrate rote memory and quickness; it does not directly address understanding of multiplication. In this sense, the quantitative standard is a proxy for understanding. This is not to say that the quantitative standard is unimportant or even less important than the qualitative one. For example, adept performance of multiplication facts requires speed as a criterion for competent performance.

Quality is in the specifications. For students to pursue competent performances, they need clear instructional goals or standards and, when appropriate, the performance assessments themselves. It is helpful for students to see a sample of the target performance, such as writing a job application letter. A sample letter provides a mental picture that the student can use as a pattern to complete the task. A description of salient features of a letter, conventions, and standards of spelling and punctuation is clearly helpful, as is an atmosphere that stresses openness to questions about the nature of the task and expectations. When students have some idea of what their target performance is or what it might look like, it is easier for them to seek assessment then when they have to guess about the performance specifications. Secrecy in testing reduces clarity of the target performance. Test specifications do not, however, need to include all elements. For example, it is appropriate to inform students that a test will cover 15 of the 50 state capitals without saying which capitals will be covered.

Quality as a relative concept suggests that improvement is more important than perfection. Although fixed standards can be important—even critical in some areas—in other areas the pursuit of quality, perhaps defined in terms of a satisfying product, may better serve students' educational needs than fixed standards. Continuous and ongoing assessment more effectively improve performance than summative testing. Useful assessment information helps students progress toward instructional goals leading to personal competence. Effective instruction then becomes that which, through sharing concepts and information, sharing criteria and standards, and sharing "tips" and shortcuts, prepares students for successful performance. In this sense, instruction and assessment are the same.

Giving and Receiving Assessment Information

Seeking assessment necessary for learning requires the capacity to give and receive assessment information. It is therefore important that students not only view assessment as a means to an end rather than as an end in itself, but that they become knowledgeable about assessment strategies and develop skill in using them. The familiar expression that the best way to learn something is by teaching it means, in part, that teaching places individuals in the position of having to know and use appropriate assessment techniques. In other words, when students provide assessment information for others or assess themselves, they must acknowledge that appropriate performance criteria, standards, and assessment strategies are key ingredients for learning. It is incumbent on teachers to help students recognize that these elements are for learning. Establishing effective assessment practices requires students to attend to performances in a constructive way. Constructive involvement in assessment means that students develop an assessment perspective that is different from traditional practice. For example, students may jointly develop their own criteria and standards, helping them divorce assessment from authority or personal feelings. In an effective learning setting, students alternate roles, sometimes giving assessment information and sometimes receiving assessment information. Potentially, this reciprocity helps alter student perceptions regarding assessment, casting it closer to learning and development rather than accountability.

Students who grow in their capacity for giving and receiving assessment increasingly come to actively participate in the assessment process. From a classroom perspective, this can be helpful to teachers who find it difficult to spend enough time for the performance review that they know to be important for learning. Student participation in the assessment process can lead to time savings for teachers and help students develop their capacity for self-assessment. The "newer" assessments, such as portfolios, do not in themselves offer any time savings; normally they require more, rather than less time. But additional assessment information accompanies students' assessment of the work of peers.

Assessment Recovery

Because assessment information is essential to the learning process, students who avoid it or are unable to use it effectively are at a severe disadvantage in school. Developing student capacity for giving and receiving assessment information and ultimately seeking assessment may often require assessment recovery. Assessment recovery is the process of rehabilitating students from a negative assessment history. Assessment experiences and recollections from childhood likely influence later reactions to assessment. Recollections that include anxiety or fear diminish opportunities for learning. Assessment experiences in the school setting may strengthen these early memories, creating a mind-set that causes students to view assessment in a negative way. Assessment viewed solely in terms of "tests," grades, and "doing well" is not likely to be something that one seeks, particularly if past experience is such that not "doing well" is a likely outcome.

Students' confidence and sense of security erode when they experience assessment primarily in negative terms. The corrective red pen points to mistakes that say, "You don't know"; "You don't understand." Without opportunity to learn from their mistakes, the red pen also says that either the performance is not important or competence is not important; students who "fail" at a task that is neither reviewed nor retaught rightfully assume that it has little value.

It is interesting that some students thrive on computer-assisted instruction. Assessment information that a computer generates is faceless, private, consistent, and, for many students, useful. Students who respond positively to a computer-assisted learning format may have had a negative assessment history; they may favor the machine because it is less likely to elicit anxiety or fears associated with past assessment experiences. Other elements unique to this assessment medium are that students can turn the assessment on or off, and the intensity of assessment responses is low for negative assessment whereas it tends to be high for positive assessment.

Changing students' views about assessment and its purpose contributes to assessment recovery. Assessment for learning greatly reduces the affective charge associated with testing. How teachers talk about assessment is equally important. For example, it is better to talk about evaluating a person's work rather than the person. Student performance evaluation is better than student evaluation, although many students have difficulty separating their performance from their person.

Finally, developing students' capacity to give and receive assessment information helps them with self-assessment. Self-assessment, not an easy task even for most adults, has inherent limitations, such as bias. Because most limitations relate to the use of assessment for purposes other than learning, self-assessment is manageable, particularly where goals, criteria, and standards are clear. In the classroom setting, even young students can, and do, practice self-assessment, for example, in reviewing their work by a set of rules, "standards," or a "key." From a classroom teacher's perspective, self-assessment by students is time efficient. But in spite of its potential as a time-saving classroom practice, its major value is to increase student independence for future learning. Self-assessment is less likely to regularly occur in classrooms where most assessment information is used summatively.

Assessment Climate

Attention directed at school climate has stressed elements related to the overall school environment. A substantial reason for addressing the school setting is the belief that young people need to feel connected to the academic mainstream, as well as to be accepted by their peers or to be members of clubs, sports groups, or music ensembles. An important element of school climate, rarely mentioned or addressed in school climate surveys, is assessment and testing. This is an unfortunate omission because students' perceived safety in seeking and using assessment information depends on the assessment climate. Creating and maintaining a safe and secure assessment climate can materially improve assessment practice. Important ingredients for assessment climate include the dimensions of assessment introduced in Chapter 1: authority, level of assessment information sought, nature of assessment information, time to use assessment information, and the tone used to convey information. Each of these has important implications for creating an appropriate assessment climate.

Students who perceive that knowledge and skills reside in the teacher (authority), experience assessment as control. When this occurs, students find themselves in opposition to the teacher. In such assessment settings, students experience rewards in response to this authority. By way of contrast, when students view information and knowledge structures as independent of the instructional leader, the teacher becomes a guiding resource, someone who can help them gain knowledge, understanding, skills, and, especially, competence. In this assessment context, students, emancipated from reacting only to the knowledge keeper, become free to seek assessment. Rather than pursue secondary rewards from the teacher, such as good grades, students can pursue affirmation of their performance. Approval thus becomes connected with their personal sense of competence rather than pleasing the teacher. Again, seeking assessment to further personal competence is the primary characteristic of effective students.

Assessment Information

Assessment plays a key role in instructional environments. In the classroom, teachers manage the use of assessment information, including whether it is formative or summative. When assessment information is routinely summative, as when used to establish grades, it loses much of its capacity to address learning in a constructive and developmental way. From the students' perspective, premature summative assessment limits safe opportunities to learn. Conversely, when instruction addresses competence, the nature and quality of information are critical and serve the formative goal of building competence.

Effective students seek assessment information as they need it to develop competence. They seek approval (affirmation) when they feel they can satisfactorily exhibit a skill or performance or when they simply need reassurance. Students rarely choose to avoid affirmation, since affirmation is always positive. But many students often avoid assessment, particularly when perhaps due to their assessment history or the assessment climate they believe that the likely outcome will be negative. A positive assessment climate can go a long way to help students who normally avoid assessment learn to value its constructive contribution.

As earlier discussed, students seek assessment at different levels of a continuum ranging from avoiding assessment to actively seeking assessment. In one learning area, students may seek or avoid assessment depending on where they are in the development of their performance. Often, due to the pace of instruction and the need to cover content, teachers force students to accept summative assessment before they are ready; when this occurs, the students' sense of competence is at risk. Valuing student competence requires that students be adequately prepared for assessment of their performance. One important consideration is whether the student is looking for assessment or affirmation.

A personal interaction with my daughter provides an illustration of a mismatch between the level of assessment sought and the level of assessment offered. She had written a story for her ninth-grade English class and came to me asking if I would like to read it, to which I replied that I would. On completing the paper, I told her I thought it was fine with a few exceptions and proceeded to offer suggestions regarding wording and punctuation. As I began to relate the first change, she took back the paper and ran from the room in tears exclaiming, "You don't like my story." In this case, this "student" was seeking affirmation, not information. The point of this anecdote is that assessment information impacts individuals personally and can be inappropriate when the timing or character of assessment information does not match the request or situation.

The nature of information given to students in the name of assessment is a critical assessment dimension. Assessment information varies in several ways that affect its usefulness for students; in some cases the kind of information dictates its use. Assessment information can simply state whether answers are right or wrong or in addition provide information about the correct answer (for missed items). Beyond this, information may be quantitative, as in percentage correct, or qualitative, as found in comments or suggestions. Information may address competence; suggestions for improvement; or affirmations, such as "Very nice work." Finally, information may reflect genuine interest in performance, such as asking questions about a paper.

As the nature of assessment information varies, so too does student response to it. How individual students react to assessment depends in large part on what they see as important. When students pursue competence, information most sought is that which affirms performance or provides guidance on how to improve performance. When the major value of assessment is its usefulness to promote learning, students need correct answers about errors. But the common tendency to attend to errors only can be dysfunctional in promoting student competence and confidence. From a competence perspective, assessment should guide students' attention toward their progress. When addressing errors, feedback should be specific and relate to students' expressed needs. Students often need help feeling comfortable enough to aggressively pursue assessment information.

Along this same line of thinking, it is prudent to help students avoid unnecessary or destructive failure. The teacher's job is to help students prepare to do well on a summative assessment activity. Testing practices should not limit students' opportunities to recover. When this situation cannot be avoided, it is helpful to balance negative judgments and provide future opportunity for students to either revise their work or, at least, to develop a rationale that leaves the student with a positive sense of capacity to learn. "Recovery" opportunities are critical for learning.

Another way, somewhat less obvious to students, that assessment information varies is in the degree to which it requires inference. For purposes here, inference means the extent that an assessment task reflects the intended performance. For example, determining whether a student can respond correctly to a factual question, such as naming the capital of Iowa, does not require inference. The student can similarly demonstrate that he or she knows that 10 times 10 is 100. In this later case, however, knowing whether or not the student understands multiplication does require inference. Conversely, students who correctly describe the process involved in multiplication understand it (low inference), but they may or may not know the multiplication tables. Level of inference becomes important for attempts to describe what students know and can do. As a rule, assessment tasks closely aligned with the intended performance require less inference than assessment tasks dissimilar to the performance.

Finally, assessment information varies in whether it relates opinions or facts. Students, particularly young students, often have a hard time differentiating between assessment based on their teacher's opinion or "objective" facts. Consequently, assessment information that is clearly opinion or preference should be so labeled. Students may perceive comments about their writing style, for example, as indicating a limitation on their part instead of a preference on the part of the teacher. In other instances, teachers may judge a students' written work as unclear or unintelligible. In the same setting, students who find a teacher's instruction unclear or unintelligible are instructed to read it again more carefully. The message these examples might send to students is that assessment relates more to authority than to knowledge.

Emotional Charge

One assessment dimension describes the emotional charge attached to assessment information. Emotional charge affects student performance because it emphasizes the personal nature of assessment. Intensity of response, either written or oral, by teachers, parents, or peers can profoundly affect students. Assessment history plays a significant role in the way students experience and the emotional charge or intensity attached to assessment information.

As an illustration of the use of intensity for communicating assessment, consider information pilots receive from air traffic controllers. For flights under instrument conditions, air traffic controllers "talk" pilots to the runway. Their job is to guide aircraft movements by providing information to pilots about their position in relation to a glide slope leading to the runway.

Their voice, calm and reassuring, affirms accurate approaches by comments such as "You are on centerline, you are on glide slope." This stock phrase communicates that the landing approach is going well. The assessment or judgment pertains to how closely the path of the aircraft parallels the one leading to the runway. If the aircraft departs from this intended path, the controller calmly informs the pilot, "You are going slightly below (or above) glide path." Only if the path of the aircraft seriously departs from the intended path will the controller's intensity change. When the aircraft is dangerously low, the voice of the controller changes dramatically in pitch and volume. The purpose of this tonal shift is to warn the pilot that immediate action is required.

The assessment elements described above directly impact students. Although the assessment practices just discussed control much of student reaction to and use of assessment, the collective setting is also important. In many respects, the collective setting refers to the general classroom climate, including the distribution of information and rewards about performance. Thus, for example, whether the classroom setting is cooperative or competitive is important, for both students and staff.

One of the most powerful contributors to general school climate is the peer group. The contribution of peers to the assessment climate is similarly strong. Peer group pressure is perhaps as great a barrier to individuals becoming effective students as is their assessment history. In particular, for students to sense safety in seeking assessment requires the absence of ridicule. In the general school climate, students who look different, act different, or have different beliefs and values can become the target of criticism. Similarly, students who make mistakes or ask questions can become targets for ridicule. The assessment impact that accompanies laughter at ideas or questions that are seriously offered can be damaging to students and restrict their learning.

Minimizing ridicule is important, particularly for students to achieve the capacity to fail. A classroom atmosphere that is warm and experienced as cooperative rather than competitive helps to establish the trust necessary for students to risk failure—and to risk learning. A warm and cooperative environment provides the foundation for a learning community that allows students to experience positive and effective assessment practices. Elements of a learning community that enhance assessment include confidentiality, openness to questions, shared information, and acceptance of diversity.

Somewhat less obviously, the assessment climate is also influenced by facilities, materials, and equipment. Students expected to achieve high-quality performances reasonably expect high-quality support. Illegible worksheets, poor seating or lighting, oversized classes, lack of learning tools (such as computers) all send the message that quality is not important. This is not to say that school districts need provide luxurious surroundings or purchase expensive equipment, but students quickly recognize inadequate materials or crowded conditions.

Finally, at least some traditional testing tends to be sterile and boring. Occasionally, this reflects the classroom environment, but more often assessment tends to represent some of the least interesting class activities. It is as if a flag goes up that says, "That completes our instruction. Now we are going to test what you have learned." When assessment is an "add-on," it is easy for students to experience one classroom climate for instruction and another climate for assessment. Such disparity in characteristics of the activity further adds to the disconnectedness that students find between assessment and instruction: Instruction is for learning; assessment is for a grade. There is no inherent reason why assessments should be any less interesting than the instruction they complement. When instruction and assessment are connected, students experience them in a similar climate. When instruction is enthusiastic and enjoyable, assessment should be also.

Concluding Comments

As stated in the 10 principles of assessment outlined in Chapter 1, everyone has the right to good assessment. We can use this principle to speak to, among other things, the issue of redress for students. Here, the right to good assessment refers not only to ways to resolve petty complaints about whether a grade should be a B+ instead of an A but rather to students' right to assessment that helps them gain competence and confidence. Clearly, inaccurate assessment, poor grading practices, or other fairness issues such as sustained bias toward individual students or student groups qualifies as poor assessment. But assessment strategies and the assessment climate, with their gross impact on students, need to be justified based on their contribution to effective learning. Experience with assessment and participation in it helps students not only recognize good assessment but also understand that teacher judgments are not infallible.

A focus on assessment to promote learning and competence does not eliminate the need for accountability. Assessment activities closely aligned to competence that students can experience—or at least perceive—provide a basis for summative assessment. Grades should connote some level of performance and students need to know what that is. Selection and placement decisions, based in part on grades, will continue, but aligning grades with competence benefits everyone. Enhancing the meaning of grades for students is served when they describe differences that students understand.

From a student competence perspective, information is needed that describes students' performances by statements and examples of what students know and can do, such as reading level, writing samples, and course completions that perhaps address general performance levels. An instructional advantage of direct measures of performance is that they allow students to concentrate their attention on instruction and assessment that helps them build competence. It is well to remember that for students, especially young students, time passes slowly and perceived change in competence is slow; consequently progress is difficult to perceive. In particular, long-term development, such as reading progress or writing skills, is not easily seen. The portfolio is an example of a collection of performance measures that over time help students see their progress.

Successful schools attend to long-term student goals. Fulfilling the goal of developing effective students can have a positive impact on students' lifelong learning. The school experience, particularly the experience with assessment, remains with students for a long time. When this experience is negative, even students at advanced levels often react in ways that run counter to the purpose of schooling. For example, it is common to see graduate students complete their dissertation and never undertake another research study due to the adverse emotional charge attached to the experience. Similarly, when school experiences result in students who rarely write again or read again or cause students to become math phobic, school has failed them. The theme of this chapter is that maintaining a susceptibility and capacity for learning is a major goal of schooling and that experience with assessment and its outcomes is critical for achieving that goal.

The development of assessment-ready students requires time as well as a supportive climate. Some—perhaps many—students can benefit from meaningful assessment recovery experiences. All students need to develop understanding and capacity to deal with a different assessment philosophy and different assessment practices. As assessment practice changes, student reactions are important, and so too is their counsel, their concerns, and their advice. Improving assessment practice requires gradual development, time, and support.

The central purpose of this chapter has been to identify assessment attributes or characteristics that describe effective students and to suggest their importance for learning. Developing assessment-ready students as well as providing a constructive assessment climate is important for learning. Helping students become assessment ready goes far beyond simply helping them be effective test takers to optimize their chances for high test scores. Throughout this chapter, I defined effective students as those capable of benefiting from good assessment information—that is, students who see assessment as a means to achieve personal competence.

If students are to become effective learners—if they are to develop competence in various academic areas, build confidence in their capacity for learning, recognize and pursue high-quality performance, and have the expectation to succeed in a variety of endeavors—then the assessment practices and the assessment climate should contribute to these desired goals.

Apart from questions regarding effective assessment practice are those that address the significance of performances assessed. What content should be covered? How much time is available for assessment?, How much high-quality work can students produce? As has been noted before, there is an intimate connection between assessment and content; content questions are also assessment questions. It is unlikely that assessment practice can be materially changed unless the curriculum also changes. Chapter 3 explores issues related to these questions.

3

CREATING A MANAGEABLE CURRICULUM

"Student competence begins with a complete performance."

One of the several planets visited by the young traveler in *The Little Prince* is inhabited only by a lamplighter (Saint-Exupery, 1943). In the course of conversation, the lamplighter relates his duty to light the lamp in the evening and put out the lamp in the morning. The pace of activity is fast since the planet turns once every minute. The little prince asks the lamplighter why he is frantically lighting and putting out the lamp. The lamplighter replies, "Those are the orders." Then he goes on,

> I follow a terrible profession. In the old days it was reasonable. I put the lamp out in the morning, and in the evening I lighted it again. I had the rest of the day for relaxation and the rest of the night for sleep.
>
> And the orders have been changed since that time? [The Little Prince replies]
>
> The orders have not been changed, said the lamplighter. That is the tragedy! From year to year the planet has turned more rapidly and the orders have not been changed! (p. 48)

Students and teachers increasingly face a plight not unlike the lamplighter's in this story. Compared with 50 years ago, there are more courses, more content in each course, and more ancillary activities to cover in no more, or perhaps less, student contact time. But "the orders have not been changed." Teachers and students must often feel like the lamplighter as they try to keep up with expanding content, a fast instructional pace, and a content mastery approach to learning that began when information was much more limited than it is now.

More textbooks with more content, in a curriculum driven by textbooks, place a strain on instruction and learning for all but the most ignited teachers and students. Even for these individuals, pressure to adhere to instruction that emphasizes a broad array of content and recall of factual information works to their disadvantage. In some cases, this instructional pace contributes to student discontent and teacher burnout. More regularly, the avalanche of content causes students to lose sight of high-quality work, makes it difficult for them to assemble information in a coherent picture, hinders their fundamental understanding of the subject, limits their long-term retention of important concepts, adds to the tedium of school, and curtails lifelong learning. In short, for many students, school lacks meaning and learning is not connected with their personal sense of competence.

Educators who recommend taking a fresh look at what students should know express concern that the content and associated pace of instruction contribute to students experiencing school without interest, memorizing isolated facts without a sense of the whole, and learning by rote without understanding. Suggestions that schools streamline their curriculum and place more emphasis on developing skills, a sense of understanding, and quality are congruent with the belief that a leaner curriculum helps students do higher-quality work and achieve a sense of personal competence. With the view that students perform better when less hurried, we should relax rather than quicken the pace of instruction. The more deliberate instructional pace that accompanies a leaner curriculum is beneficial in part because it expands possibilities for assessment procedures and use of an assessment process directed at student competence in valued knowledge and skills.

As more content has been covered, more assessment has been added. Assessment practice, in the interest of efficiency and objectivity, increasingly has come to rely on methods amenable to covering extensive content. Assessment formats such as multiple choice, short answer, and, more recently, machine-scored tests have become dominant assessment tools. These formats are popularly used to address curriculum that emphasizes factual content; thus they reflect an excellent match between curriculum and assessment. Classroom assessment practices that rely on formats such as multiple-choice, true-false, and short answer questions, efficiently assess students' grasp of factual material. Essays, performance assessments, and portfolios have multiple strengths, but efficient and objective scoring are not among them. Consequently, in the absence of a shift away from emphasis on content at the knowledge level, simply changing from one assessment method to another is likely to be counterproductive.

When teachers are confronted with constraints beyond their control, such as an expanding curriculum, efficiently obtained and easily defended assessment information for uses external to the student become the norm. Teachers justifiably protest prescriptions to alter their assessment practice unless accompanied by serious curriculum review. They appropriately ask, "How much of the curriculum can *we assess* in ways that are meaningful?" The answer to this question begins with two others: "How much of the curriculum is meaningful and which elements of the curriculum are most meaningful?" and "If we cannot meaningfully assess the curriculum, can students meaningfully learn it?"

When teachers find themselves racing to complete the book by the end of the year or to fight the Civil War by Thanksgiving, what does this signal to our students? Hastening to ensure we "get done" can lead to superficial instruction and superficial assessment. What value does assessment information have to students who want to improve their performance if there is no time to use it? Why should students seek assessment information if they do not have opportunity to use it? Is high-quality work or student competence a likely outcome under these conditions? How quickly can we and our students "light and put out the lamp"? Or should the orders be changed?

The focus for this chapter is to discuss a review process to connect a meaningful curriculum and student competence through effective instruction and assessment. A review process is introduced as a way to connect instructional and assessment goals. This process points to the value of plans to guide instruction and assessment and an assessment portfolio to weigh the impact they have on students. Finally, implications of the review process are discussed along with a note about standards. The emphasis throughout this chapter is on the point that the interplay between curriculum, instruction, and assessment directs what students know and what they can do.

Curriculum, Instruction, Assessment, and Competence

A curriculum contains general aims that prescribe or imply student competence. Instruction and assessment are the means by which students become competent in the curriculum. Students come to know the curriculum through instruction and assessment; they experience instruction and assessment frequently and intensely but rarely encounter the curriculum. Teachers control instruction and assessment but not the curriculum and student competence. Teachers did not invent geometry; nor can they make students learn it. Teachers' responsibility and authority for learning begin and end with instruction and assessment. Teachers are not responsible for the curriculum; nor are they solely responsible for student competence. Clearly, however, a teacher's primary duty is to help students become competent. Recognizing the limits of teachers' responsibilities speaks to their role in review process. Once the curriculum is established, teachers must align their instruction with it and align assessments with instruction. The assessment process could be aligned directly with the curriculum, but as a practical matter it is more efficiently aligned with instruction. Because assessment information guides student learning, the fit between curriculum and instruction should be as close as possible. When that fit is exact, assessment aligned with instruction is also aligned with the curriculum. The importance of connecting curriculum with

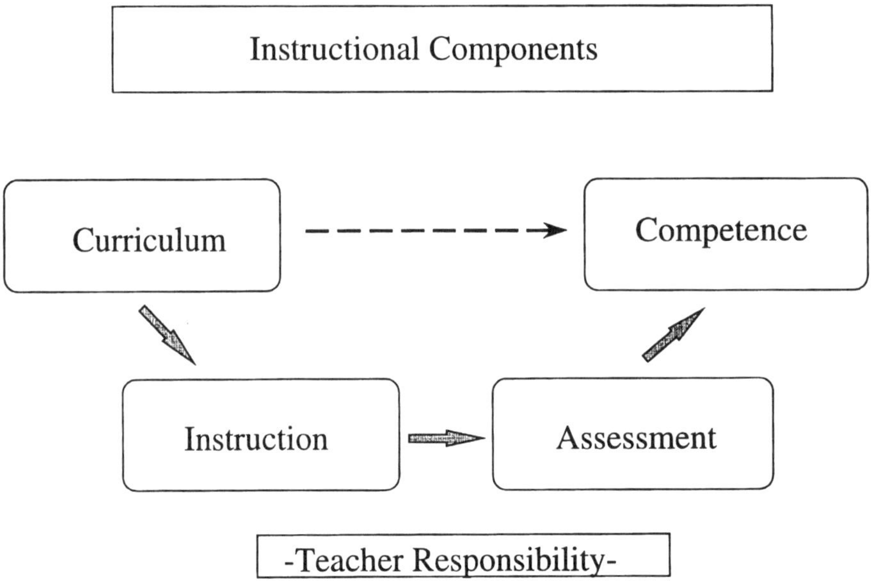

Figure 3.1. Instructional Components

assessment points out that students' experience with assessment identifies what the real curriculum is. Assessment tells students what their teachers believe is important to learn.

Curriculum Components

We have mentioned connections between curriculum, instruction, assessment, and competence. We return to those connections now to describe a process for moving curriculum into the classroom. The four instructional components are as follows:

- *Curriculum* establishes the general aims for students and goals for instruction.
- *Instruction* is the means employed to teach the curriculum. It provides learning opportunities in the way of exercises, activities, readings, and information that help students achieve the expressed curriculum goals. Instruction is what teachers orchestrate.
- *Assessment* provides information about how well students are doing in achieving the curriculum goals. Assessment activities provide students with opportunities to interact with the curriculum in meaningful ways.
- *Competence* in the curriculum is the aim of teaching.

Figure 3.1 shows the connection between the curriculum and student competence, reflecting the belief that the purpose of schooling is to develop students who are competent. Curriculum limitations and slippage between connecting elements of the learning process diminish the value of schooling for students. *Slippage* refers to the difference between actual student competence and curriculum goals. First, the curriculum may not address valued learnings. Curriculum goals can be irrelevant or insufficient to student needs. For example, failure to prepare students in technology may represent an insufficient curriculum. Slippage can occur between curriculum and instruction when instruction does not address curricular goals. A curriculum goal may be to develop students' use of computer technology to solve mathematics problems. Instruction limited to keyboarding and basic computer literacy does not address this curriculum goal.

Differences between instructional goals and activities and assessment tasks represent another source of misalignment that has received much attention by persons touting alternative forms of assessment. A common example is when instruction addresses complex ideas or higher-order thinking skills but subsequent assessment procedures tap only factual knowledge. Finally, limited student competence in the curriculum may result from students being either unable or unwilling to use assessment information to build competence. Students may lack time to adequately use assessment information, the information they receive may be inadequate to modify their performance, or they may simply choose to ignore the information.

The purpose of the overall curriculum-assessment review process, beginning with the curriculum, is to minimize the slippage between curricular goals and student competence. Because the emphasis of this book is assessment, a critical review element is to examine how well assessment practices align with instructional outcomes and how well assessment helps students achieve competence in areas identified as important. Students' most direct experience with the curriculum comes at the point of assessment, specifically when it affirms a complete or competent performance.

Defining student competence in terms of the curriculum requires that curricular and instructional aims be aligned. Although teachers' responsibility for student learning begins and ends with instruction and assessment, it is their charge to provide instruction that parallels the curriculum and assessment information that helps students become competent in it. Even though teachers do not govern student competence, it is their primary duty to nurture it. At a basic level, the curriculum consists of skills such as reading, writing, and mathematics; decision making skills; and social skills, but more generally it includes any performance that students can experience as complete. When competent performance is the goal of instruction, students need to know what it is and when it happens. We need therefore to communicate curriculum goals to students using tasks or complete performances, such as reading a book, tying a shoe, multiplying fractions, or participating in a group activity. These complete performances become instructional goals in which assessment plays a crucial role. Initial assessments supply information that helps students achieve complete performances. Subsequent assessment practices convey information *students* can use to become competent or to know when they are competent.

A Meaningful Curriculum

The pace of instruction depends on content, criteria, standards, and assessment. We can "change the orders"—that is, establish a leaner and more meaningful curriculum, by exercising control over these four instructional elements. A leaner curriculum does not mean one of lower quality or one that is less rigorous. It does mean one consisting of valued content, appropriate criteria and standards, and effective assessment practices.

Curriculum review provides opportunity to cull the curriculum of elements that no longer serve students needs, to add new curriculum that does serve students (e.g., technology), and to acknowledge that some content and some criteria are more important than others. Taken together, these elements govern the pace of instruction, which in turn affects the quality of work and the value of assessment information to promote it. The content dimension describes what knowledge and skills are important and includes indications about which are more important than others. Criteria, the second dimension, describe elements that constitute a complete performance. Standards add specificity to the criteria for complete or competent performances. We often cast standards in the language of developmentally appropriate objectives that address complexity of performances, such as paragraph length. Finally, assessment activities speak to curriculum issues by imposing learning requirements on students. For example, assessment formats dictate whether students need to recall factual information or recognize correct answers.

Content, criteria, and standards all contribute to the pace of instruction. The amount of content affects teachers and students alike; criteria and standards more directly affect students. The pace of instruction warrants concern because the first casualties of a fast pace are student competence and high-quality work. As we propose content, criteria, and standards, we need to weigh their impact on students. Assessment tasks describe what students must do. How many tasks we ask them to do, the expectations for each (such as the amount of material to cover), whether or not elements need to be memorized, whether students need to supply correct answers or recognize them, and whether we expect them to achieve a high standard of performance all make a difference for students.

Meaningful Content

Consequential and difficult questions attend the process of curriculum review to promote student competence. Questions needing answers include, What student competencies do we most value? What instructional issues are most important? What prerequisite skills and knowledge are essential building blocks for more advanced topics? What skills do students need to perform successfully? What performance elements help students experience competence? What student limitations are acceptable? Answers to these questions lie in content areas and are not within the scope of this book. But answers to these questions provide initial direction for attending to assessment issues. Although this book is not about curricula or their development, connecting assessment with curriculum is important. Curriculum and how it is defined affects assessment practices.

Discussions about curriculum often reflect the tension between two dimensions, breadth and depth. Review of curriculum and assessment practices has to address this difficult but essential issue. Consequently, we must decide how much subject matter development, depth, and higher-order thinking we want compared to breadth of content. The curriculum can emphasize highly specified objectives and complete performances and activities that call for application and use of concepts in ways that build students' sense of competence. Competence implies that students can use knowledge and skills in ways that are meaningful or useful. Given this premise, it is appropriate to design the curriculum for complete performances wherever possible. Doing so is likely to result in fewer objectives and a leaner curriculum.

Factual Information

There continue to be important facts that students need to know. Some of these stand alone, such as simple addition facts, whereas other factual information serves as building blocks for more advanced topics. Facts that are important in their own right or as building blocks for other learning taken alone, do not sufficiently define a complete performance. Some exceptions occur, such as the performance of counting to 10. Unit tests and end-of-course tests that place singular emphasis on the recall or recognition of somewhat isolated pieces of information do not do justice to instruction that in addition to factual material covers broad concepts and emphasizes application or synthesis of information. When overemphasized, facts lead to boredom and students lose sight of the curriculum. This is not meant to imply a fact-free curriculum, but rather the need to include or exclude factual material on the basis of its relative merit in the curriculum. Assessment activities can then include knowledge of facts in the context of a complete performance.

Selecting factual information as appropriate content is one outcome of a comprehensive review of curriculum. Individual topic reviews weigh points of fact in terms that address their importance. Some facts are essential, such as knowing simple addition combinations. Other factual information may be important, but not essential, such as the location of Norway. Finally, many facts are of only passing interest or valued for promoting general awareness, such as the date Magellan sailed around the world. The primary review outcome is delineating what is important for students to know and why. Beyond teachers knowing what is important from an instructional perspective is student awareness of what is important. Knowledge of important factual material presented in the context of a complete performance helps students know what is important and how it fits into a larger picture.

Meaningful Criteria and Standards

Effective review of curriculum, instruction, and assessment hinges on the distinction between criteria and standards. Making this distinction explicit helps us build curricula to guide instruction and assessment in ways that are meaningful for students. Criteria tend to be more stable than standards or expectations. Once again, the distinction between a complete performance and a competent one is useful. Complete performances are described in terms of criteria; competent ones are defined in terms of standards. Almost everyone will argue that standards should be set high. Lowering performance standards slows the pace of instruction but is clearly not recommended. What is important, however, is that reasonable standards be set. Controlling standards means setting them as high as is practical. The criteria we choose to apply to a performance may offer a better mechanism to control the pace of instruction than standards do. A simple example illustrates these two levels of performance. In track and field, athletes may compete in the standing high jump that describes the performance. They achieve a *complete performance* by jumping over the bar. The competitive standard is the (defined) height of the bar. They achieve a *competent* performance by reaching or exceeding the competitive standard.

The value of complete performances is that they simultaneously direct our attention to the learner and to the curriculum. Complete performances describe the curriculum in terms that students can experience or at least see. As an example, suppose an instructional goal is that students learn addition. The initial complete performance is to grasp the meaning of addition. When we communicate this essential goal, correctly adding two numbers, and affirm its occurrence, we provide students with the sense of knowing the concept of addition, a true accomplishment. Once students acquire the concept of addition, they are ready to develop facility with it, such as adding all single-digit numbers or adding 100 single-digit numbers in 10 minutes. The timed performance represents an added criterion, namely speed. It is important for students, however, to recognize the difference between criteria or standards that go beyond the initial complete performance, understanding addition, and extended performance criteria or standards. Students develop facility with addition by addressing limitations in their performances, such as improving speed and accuracy. We serve students well when we help them address limitations in secondary criteria or standards without detracting from their initial accomplishment.

Moving beyond understanding addition to facility with it, let us assume that a student correctly answers 85 of 100 addition problems in 10 minutes and the assessment information he or she receives is the summary score of 85%. The value of this information increases if it communicates student accomplishments and areas that need improvement. The two criteria in this example are speed and accuracy, and the respective standards are completing 100 problems in 10 minutes at 100% accuracy. The student who completes only 85 problems, but correctly answers all 85, apparently knows addition,

TABLE 3.1 Characteristics of Competent Performances

Competent Performance More Than a Complete One	*Competent Performance Less Than or Equal to a Complete One*
Example: Writing a letter	Examples: Knowing the state capitals, Counting to 10
Little direction	Highly specified
Open-ended	Constrained
Higher-order objectives	Lower-order objectives
Process	Content/procedures
Developmental/drafts	Nondevelopmental/practice
Criteria/expectations	Standards
Complete and competent performances emerge	Complete and competent performances specified
Style open	Style restrained
Multiple "correct" answers	Correct answers specified

but did not or could not finish all 100 problems. It is important that the student recognize that he or she knows addition facts but may need to address speed. Alternatively, students who attempt all 100 problems, but incorrectly answer 15 of them, may need to review their addition facts. This example illustrates that the value of assessment activities depends on the kind of information provided and highlights the critical role played by criteria and standards for student learning. It is important that such criteria are valid in terms of the curriculum. The same idea applies to memorizing formulas, neatness, and speed.

A complete performance and a competent one may be the same. The complete performance of counting to 10 reflects competence by its being completed. But complete performances and competent ones are frequently not the same. A competent performance may be more or less than a complete one. Characteristics of competent performances vary depending on whether they are more or less than complete ones. Table 3.1 provides a summary of characteristics that distinguish between competent performances that are more than complete ones and competent performances that are less than or equal to complete ones.

Writing a letter can serve as an example of a complete performance that is less than a competent one. Consider a letter written by Amy, a first-grade student, to her grandmother (see Figure 3.2). This letter has multiple errors in spelling, punctuation, grammar, and letter formation. It is far from a competent performance for adults or advanced students. It is, however, a complete performance because it communicates a message, in writing, to another person.

A complete performance also may be more than a competent one. If we ask students to name the 50 state capitals, the complete performance is to

Monday

dear Grandma

Thanks for the cookies

I luv you.

Amy

Figure 3.2. Amy's Letter

correctly name all 50. But a student achieves a competent performance that is less than complete when the standard is to recall only 45 of the total set of 50 capitals. A complete performance that is less than a competent one is expansive and developmental. Conversely, a complete performance that is more than a competent one is constrained.

Adding or deleting criteria has a substantial impact on performances. For example, the complete performance of adding single-digit numbers implies the criterion of accuracy. If we subsequently define a competent performance as adding 100 pairs of single-digit numbers in 10 minutes, the criteria have changed, resulting in a competence standard that goes beyond the original complete performance. Speed is a frequently used criterion that may have a legitimate basis in the curriculum; in the present example, day-to-day use of addition requires some or even considerable facility. But from students' perspective, premature attention to quickness can diminish their deserved sense of competence in adding numbers; it is helpful to affirm students' initial complete performances before introducing additional criteria and standards.

Criteria, such as speed, are appropriate when they reflect performance characteristics that are important in practicality, such as making change. It is less obvious that speed is a relevant criterion for completing long division problems. Speed is commonly a factor in assessment tasks and one that usually results in performance differences. Consider again the performance running a marathon. The time required to run this distance ranges from just over 2 hours to many hours. In a world-class race, the performance range might be only minutes. The criterion for most people who run marathons is endurance, not speed; most run to complete the race, not to win it. Speed plays an increasingly larger role for runners who have built confidence in their endurance. The point is not that those who race marathons and lose or those who simply run them are not competent, but that the speed standard does not do justice to the completed performance. The curriculum issue is whether speed is a relevant performance criterion, thereby deserving of some real-world standard, or whether it simply serves to identify performance differences. Examinations that cover a substantial amount of material in a restricted time limit are like a competitive marathon in that results depend on endurance and speed.

Criteria not aligned with the curriculum add needlessly to it and thereby needlessly quicken the pace of instruction. Permitting or denying students use of reference materials or calculators is another criterion that often attends assessment. Requiring students to memorize information or formulas has the effect of adding to the curriculum. Memorization is a criterion, not a standard. When we require students to solve problems using formulas it makes a real difference whether or not they must have the formulas committed to memory. From students' perspective, this is an issue efficiency and instructional pace because committing formulas to memory requires a substantial amount of time. We need to justify memorization on the basis of whether or not it has practical meaning in the curriculum. For example, asking students in an introductory statistics class to demonstrate their capacity to compute a correlation coefficient without access to the formula to complete it goes beyond a valid curriculum unless we can envision an employer request such as, "Please compute the correlation coefficient between costs and sales, but do not use a reference or computational device."

Competence standards supply clues about the importance attached to the performance. We acknowledge the importance of safety, for example, by setting a "zero tolerance" standard. Procedures and rules that govern operation of power equipment fall in this category. Critical skills or knowledge similarly rest on zero tolerance standards. Counting to 10, knowing the alphabet, and spelling basic words are simple examples. Frequently, standards are set arbitrarily, such as 70% correct for a passing score. Such standards treat all performances the same or allow performances to vary as long as they average out to 70%. Scores based on assessment activities may over- or underestimate competence when we apply a 70% standard for multiple tasks that vary in difficulty or performance conditions. That all performances have the same percentage basis for competence is at odds with the curriculum. Tying criteria and standards to the curriculum allows us to set "competence" levels that vary in terms of the task difficulty. For some curriculum areas, 40% may denote a satisfactory level of competence or point to an emerging competence.

Criteria and Technology

Technology has exerted a major impact on the curriculum. Technology has a curriculum of its own and thus adds substantial learning tasks to the schooling experience. But technology such as calculators, computers, and information and retrieval systems can also reduce the curriculum. Considerable differences exist in the knowledge and skills needed to complete tasks with or without a calculator or computer. For example, calculators and computers moderate individual speed and accuracy standards for arithmetic and computational skills and offer students opportunity to access complex mathematical concepts without the tedium of completing the operations they require. Technology similarly serves writing. Word processing programs, for example, routinely include software to check spelling and grammar. In addition to being an aid to writing, these features can be instructive in their own right, as when students use technology to correct spelling. The application of technology does not mean that students no longer need to learn to spell or to do arithmetic computations. But the availability and capacity of calculators and computers have implications for curricular criteria and standards that address the pace of instruction. Building important conceptual ideas in terms of complete performances is often easier when students are allowed to bypass the tedium that may accompany their use.

Review of Instruction and Assessment

The purpose for curriculum review is to guide instruction and assessment practices that are student centered. In particular, assessment of instructional goals needs to be aligned with curriculum and lead to student competence. Defining the curriculum in terms of complete performances acknowledges that these are the initial step toward competence; competence begins with a complete performance. Initial assessment information helps students achieve a complete performance; ongoing assessment helps them become competent. Students need assessment information to affirm their complete performances. The complete performance is the student's first glimpse of the curriculum.

Curriculum review by local education agencies begins with general education goals defined in terms of mission and policy. These broad aims often include general curriculum goal statements and a systematic and periodic review of them. Guidelines such as content standards produced by national professional organizations influence local or state curricula. Examples of such guidelines include the National Council of Teachers of Mathematics (1989) *Curricular and Evaluation Standards for School Mathematics* and the American Association for the Advancement of Science (1993) *Benchmarks of Science Literacy*. At the local level, curriculum describes specific subject matter content, often in course offerings at upper grade levels. More detailed reviews focus on particular courses of study. Individual teachers, a specified group of teachers, or all teachers in a particular subject may complete this review. Content standards, such as those just mentioned, are useful resources for curriculum reviews.

Curriculum reviews result in statements of general goals for students. It is important that curriculum goals be sufficiently described to guide instruction. Once curriculum statements are in place, the review process continues with instructional and assessment planning. These critical reviews, accomplished by teachers, connect instruction with the curriculum and assessment with instruction; instruction and assessment are the mechanisms by which students become competent in the curriculum. Instruction and assessment are dynamic processes; the curriculum is not. Maintaining alignment of instruction and assessment with the curriculum is an ongoing challenge for teachers, one with several potential obstacles. Examples of obstacles include outdated textbooks that inadequately cover important topics, differences between *student* understanding of curricular goals and instructional objectives and assessment policies, and practices that do not accommodate the dynamics of effective instruction. Overcoming obstacles that contribute to curriculum slippage and limit learning requires an ongoing review process, such as the general model described in Chapter 1. There, I suggested that review of instruction and assessment begins by looking beneath our practices to the beliefs, attitudes, and values we hold and beyond our practices to the impact they have on students. A supportive climate that allows teachers to safely review and revise their professional practice enhances the process. Initially, teachers need permission to explore instruction and assessment issues in the confines of their classroom in conjunction with colleagues; they also need the authority and support to pursue this professional process.

Ongoing review consists of cautious exploration and implementation of instruction and assessment practices that help students learn and achieve competence. It is accomplished one assessment task at a time. Taking direction from the general model, the emphasis is to examine the impact instruction and assessment practices have on student learning. Curriculum takes on form and substance at the point of instruction and assessment—in the classroom where teachers and students interact. These interactions offer teachers information that signals the need to redefine a complete performance, add or delete a performance criterion, change the instructions to complete an assessment activity, or expand the time allotted to complete a unit.

As a practical matter, connecting the curriculum, instruction, assessment, and competence requires three products: an instructional plan, commonly known as a lesson plan; an assessment plan that describes assessment activities and procedures; and an assessment portfolio. Lesson plans and assessment activities already in place provide the bases for instructional and assessment plans. The assessment portfolio, maintained by teachers, helps to monitor the impact of instruction and assessment practices. The portfolio accommodates information about the outcomes of teachers' practices and encourages reflective practice based on teachers' judgments and those of colleagues and students. Because assessment for learning is an ongoing process, the assessment portfolio is an active document.

The goal of the assessment review process is simply to connect instructional plans that describe what teachers do with assessment plans that describe what students do. An assessment plan should provide information that describes student learnings or performances. The plan needs to communicate these performances in sufficient detail for students to gain a picture of the task, either in words they can understand or by samples they can see; in short, it needs to communicate what students are striving for in terms of personal competence. Clearly communicating complete performances to students is essential to integrate instruction and assessment with curricular and instructional aims. A positive assessment climate allows students to ask clarifying questions about the performance task or permits them to safely complete an initial performance, such as a draft, that can later be modified. Learning goals are often listed or categorized using terminology such as Bloom's taxonomy: knowledge, comprehension, application, analysis, synthesis, and evaluation (Bloom, Englehart, Furst, Hill, & Krathwohl, 1956). An effective assessment plan provides information teachers can use to help students recognize complete and competent performances.

Curriculum and assessment review do not imply discarding what is currently in place and starting over; what is in place becomes the starting point. Teachers will likely retain most instructional, or lesson, plans and instructional approaches. The review process simply seeks to define—or redefine—the curriculum from a student's perspective by establishing instructional priorities and then determining how to assess these priorities in ways that help students learn and that lead them to experience competence. The purpose of the process is to identify or combine objectives as complete performances. The number of instructional objectives will not necessarily decrease, although the process of establishing priorities may eliminate some and diminish the importance of others.

Instructional Plans

Instructional plans begin with stated meaningful complete performances followed by delineation of supporting objectives and activities that lead to them. Complete performances help students see connections among instructional elements and supporting objectives and processes. All instructional objectives are not complete performances, but they should all lead to complete performances. For example, diagramming sentences contributes to students' writing skills but is not itself an instructional goal. Ancillary skills, such as diagramming sentences, are parallel and helpful elements to enhance complete performances, in this case writing. The curriculum may not require students to diagram sentences, but it may be instructionally valid to do so if it promotes student competence with respect to what the curriculum does require.

Many schools have meticulously specified teaching objectives for many subject areas. From a teacher's perspective, this level of specificity may be helpful. But is it helpful for *students?* Does specification of large numbers of instructional objectives carry the message of where instruction is taking *them?* The power of assessment to direct student learning requires that assessment activities be developed from their perspective. Instruction, assessment, and student performance become connected through the use of an assessment plan and assessment portfolio.

Assessment Plans

Assessment connects student activities with student competence. Translating instructional goals into assessment goals calls for an assessment plan that is an extension of the lesson plan. The assessment plan describes performances that follow from instruction and delineate significant aspects of assessment tasks, such as what students do, what information they receive, and when they receive it. Complete performances and the assessment information that attends them unite instruction and assessment with curricular or instructional aims. Assessment plans are lesson plans seen from a student's perspective.

The assessment plan serves as a guide for developing assessment products and activities; it has a long history in formal test development. Assessment plans, often referred to as test specification tables or test blueprints, help test developers ensure that tests systematically cover a broad array of content. In the classroom, the purpose is to aid translation of instructional objectives into assessment activities that promote student competence and facilitate articulation in the subject and from grade to grade.

The assessment planning process begins with current practice. An initial examination of instructional aims and associated assessment activities should reveal whether or not they are congruent. Assessment review examines the extent to which assessment procedures and activities address students' competence. Reviews limited to instructional goals only address plans not actions. Unit-by-unit review of student activities, assessment information, and performances help teachers see the curriculum as students see it. From this point of view, student feedback on assessment procedures and the information they provide is useful.

Assessment plans can take many forms, depending on personal preference; the format is only important to the extent that it serves to connect assessment activities with instruction and student performance. A commonly used format lists instructional objectives and suggests emphasis about the nature of assessment tasks in terms of some conceptual structure, such as Bloom's taxonomy (Bloom et al., 1956). Use of this common format initially serves to identify content. It also provides a basis for setting instructional priorities and can help frame complete performances. A sample content specification of the assessment plan is shown in Table 3.2.

Assessment as a process requires an assessment plan that goes beyond content specification. For classroom use, assessment plans require more than an ordinary list of test objectives. The complete assessment plan calls for effective application of assessment activities, including allotting time for students to use information, description of the assessment information provided students, and opportunities for review and revision. Of special interest are instructional priorities that define or combine instructional objectives as complete performances. Students benefit from examples of performances and knowing what the complete performance is. Descriptions or examples of complete performances provide such pictures and should

TABLE 3.2 Sample Assessment Plan Content Specification

Topic	*Knowledge & Comprehension*	*Application & Analysis*	*Synthesis & Evaluation*	*Priority*
Basic Assessment Concepts	Vocabulary	Journal	Develop opinion and consider implications	1
Formal Assessment Characteristics	Vocabulary	Use appropriately	Contrast	1
Table of Specifications	Identify components	Develop for a topic of interest	Critique own and colleagues'	1
Paper and Pencil Test Protocols	Identify types	Develop for topic	Critique own and colleagues'	1
Performance Assessment	List characteristics	Develop for topic	Critique own and colleagues'	1
Journal/Portfolio		Develop for course learnings		2
Published Tests	Recognize components	Review	Critique	2
Norm- and Criterion-Referenced Assessment	Compare	Differentiate	Assess implications	1

include information about the purpose of the activity, criteria, and standards (when appropriate). Specification of complete performances helps assessment activities achieve "face validity"—that is, one purpose of specifying complete performances is to encourage students to engage the curriculum and students are more likely to do so when activities make sense to them and they can recognize or experience a complete or competent performance. A note of caution is in order here. Overspecification for some tasks may detract from the richness of performances. Activities that call for argumentation using supporting facts, connections among those facts, or active or creative solutions may lose some of the vitality and purposefulness when constrained by too much specification. The assessment plan will be revisited in the next chapter.

The Teacher's Personal Assessment Portfolio

Assessment portfolios, maintained by teachers, are vehicles used to monitor and review instruction and assessment practices. Entries for the assessment portfolio include information about the general topic, assessment goals, the nature of the performance or task to be completed, copies of assessment activities, criteria and standards, scoring procedures, information that assessment should provide students, and as it becomes available information about the impact of the assessment in achieving desired goals. Assessment portfolios allow teachers to reflect on instructional and assessment plans and the interplay between them.

Student assessment exercises become part of the assessment portfolio and an integral part of instructional plans. The teacher assessment portfolio is simply a vehicle to record and examine assessment practices and to alter assessments to make them more effective, if necessary. The portfolio is an active document, containing not only assessment activities and their results but also judgments about assessments (such as their impact), examined summaries of student results (where appropriate), and collegial review. Obtaining information about the effectiveness of instruction and assessment reflects a professional level of concern about the impact teaching has on students. The teacher's personal assessment portfolio is taken up in the next chapter and a sample portfolio is provided in Appendix A.

Review of assessment practice in the classroom is not a trivial task or one readily or quickly accomplished across multiple topics or objectives. Producing assessment information that supports high-quality student performances requires time. In particular, quality assessments require time to plan and reflect on information about their application and usefulness in achieving stated instructional goals.

The importance of a professional climate, one conducive to collegial interchange and support for staff, cannot be overstated. High-quality work is important for this endeavor if it is ultimately to promote work of similar quality on the part of students; the intent is to proceed deliberately but at a comfortable pace. In addition, teacher competence and confidence are likely to result from positive student assessment experiences. This sense of accomplishment, affirmed through collegial support and student learning, is a professional reward that educators should routinely experience.

Implications

I have discussed a curriculum review process that suggests some general things to accomplish. Irrespective of the specific strategy or procedure, the purpose is to address the complementary issues of priority of curricular goals, the pace of instruction, and the quality of work. The review process itself adheres to these same general ideas; it should first address areas of most priority, be of high quality, and be completed at a reasonable pace. The review process can and should begin with current practices and build on successful ones; many instructional and assessment practices do achieve desired goals. But when current practices are not effective, teachers need to revise them. Doing so will require time and patience. The task of reviewing and altering instruction and assessments must proceed deliberately, one topic at a time.

Several implications follow from this review process. Assessment review helps affirm core learning goals; prioritize content, including factual material that affects the pace of instruction; expand students' capacity to use assessment information; and help them produce high-quality work. Review of curriculum goals and instructional objectives identify valued knowledge and skills in subject areas. The process helps define competence and complete performances in ways that help *students know* what teachers wish for them and of them. It also provides occasion to address the relative value of objectives and content found in textbooks or other instructional materials. Local review asks us to define what we value for students in *our* community and *our* classrooms.

Teachers' involvement in the review process encourages reflective practice. Teaching toward complete performances and competency requires more guidance and less direction, more coaching and fewer instructions, and more information that students can use to build competence and less information that serves external needs. A significant outcome of attending to classroom assessment is to once again connect assessment with student and teacher needs rather than to requirements outside the classroom. Assessment is most powerful when used to build or affirm competence. The value of student assessment lies in the information it delivers to students and teachers. For students, assessment information helps them know what they need to improve and when they have achieved competence. Similarly, for teachers, assessment information points to needed changes in instruction or affirms when it has been effective. Aspects of student performance vary in quality, novelty, creativity, efficiency, and so forth, but teachers affirm their instructional effort in terms of individual student learning, aggregated by competent or complete performances. The amount of content and use of criteria extraneous to the performance contribute to a dysfunctional pace that constrains instruction, limits competence, and robs teachers of a major source of personal satisfaction. A more deliberate pace, on the other hand, expands connections between student competence, professional confidence, and instructional rewards for teachers.

Review of curriculum and instruction includes consideration of whether the curriculum best serves diverse students needs. Maintaining students' interests in achieving competence and instilling confidence in their ability to learn are what lead to success stories that occur late in the school experience or even after the school experience. Curriculum and assessment experiences that develop learning capacity, such as reading skills, while maintaining interest in performance and competence serve students well.

Who writes the basic curriculum to guide instruction is not as important as that its elements are sufficiently clear to guide instruction. A curriculum that is meaningful for teachers contributes to instruction that is meaningful for students. A meaningful curriculum-instruction match depends on professionalism, commitment to the curriculum goals and objectives, and the availability of support mechanisms to allow it to flourish in the classroom. If the curriculum is not clear, teachers need to ask about it; if they are not committed to its goals, they need to determine why; and if support mechanisms are insufficient for its successful transfer to students, they need to request adequate support.

The appeal of performance standards is that they imply performance levels achieved through an iterative learning process. In this sense, they are preferred over learning "objectives." Standards can serve to focus the curriculum toward more general tasks and goals and be student centered. National standards serve as a useful guide and resource for this process. But minimal standards need not be a system target or a teaching target. The target should be personal best for all students. Minimum standards for accountability may be similar to minimum standards for a complete performance; advanced standards are goals for student competence.

In the assessment framework proposed in this book, we do not raise standards by adding content or more courses. A major goal of curriculum review in terms of student performance is to address the issues of quality and quantity. From a student performance perspective, raising standards means increasing levels of competence, not adding content.

The focus on a single set of specific outcomes suggests that one set can serve all students equally. Content and performance standards and other attempts to define schooling in specific and singular terms have limited value because they do not account for diversity in communities and diversity in students. Communities benefit by developing a clear sense of what they want their students to know and be like; each needs to decide. No other part of the assessment process is more important—or more difficult. Students need to know what is important. Students discover that important topics are those reviewed and retaught.

What students should know and what they should be able to do requires a look at the future, not the past. In years past, parents and grandparents of today's students were, for the most part, taught subjects in a way that placed emphasis on limited factual material and memorization. We know that parents and grandparents persevered with the skills they attained in the schools of their day. But, as with the lamplighter, our world has changed. Not only is there more information than in the past, but there are also significant changes in the way information is processed (technology), the nature of work (robotics), and requirements for cooperative work behavior. Whether from postsecondary institutions or the business community, calls for changing the way students are educated emphasize producing students who can write better, think better, learn better, and adapt better. We need to frame curriculum, instruction, and assessment in ways that address these general learner skills.

4

Using Assessment Information Effectively

"Assessment information is effective as received, not as given."

Because assessment information powerfully affects student attitudes, behavior, and learning, assessment practice warrants consideration, planning, and investment of time. In previous chapters, I noted that assessment purpose and instructional goals drive the selection or development of assessment methods. The assessment practices teachers use, driven by goals and purposes that are often implicit, impact students in particular ways. Because assessment is an integral part of effective instruction, teachers need to be skilled in its use. One of the professional duties of teachers is to select and develop assessment methods appropriate for their purposes. Teachers are professional critics duty bound to constructively assess students' performances. Sound decisions about classroom assessment hinge on teachers' repertoire of assessment methods and their facility with the assessment process.

In spite of their powerful effects on students and central role in instruction, classroom assessment practices and procedures have been neglected in comparison to other elements of instruction. Teacher training in assessment is absent or deficient and support for research in classroom assessment is meager (Gullickson, 1986). Limited assessment training and experience coupled with testing requirements external to the classroom constrain assessment practice. These limitations restrict the professional prerogative regarding assessment and disconnect it from instruction.

Teachers routinely provide assessment for learning as a natural part of their instruction, particularly when assessment is informal. Day-to-day classroom assessment activities include hundreds of instances of teachers guiding, directing, and offering suggestions to students about learning objectives. But pressures to cover the content often limit the flexibility of formal assessments suited to address the total range of learning objectives. Standardized test scores receive much attention, are highly visible, and often involve high stakes for students, teachers, and school districts. Educators are pressed to tailor their instruction to address the demands of such tests and shape their assessment practices to fit the test characteristics. Assessment for learning also pales in comparison to so-called high-stakes assessment—that is, assessment directly tied to selection or accountability decisions. In short, the perspective that often drives assessment practices is that tests are for selection and accountability.

The limited time for assessment coupled with the convenience of assessment formats that are quick to score also restrict the assessment process. Scoring efficiency is important when tests cover a substantial number of objectives for use with large numbers of students. The ongoing assessment practices that promote learning, including higher-order objectives, require more information and different information than those that address selection or accountability. In short, assessment as a means to an end is far different from assessment as an end in itself.

Assessment for Learning

Schools provide students with opportunities to learn through a cyclic process of instruction and assessment activities. The assessment part of the cycle places students in performance settings that inform them about their progress, including information about what they can do to improve it. The characteristics, qualities, and criteria of assessment practices that are first and foremost for students encourage them to participate in the assessment process. Student participation in assessment increases its efficiency, permits teachers to shed their perceived responsibility for the curriculum and student competence, and suggests more effective assessment criteria.

Leading the list of benefits for assessment practices focused on students is their participation in the evaluative process. Evaluation of work in comparison to specified criteria is essential for learning; students can and should become skilled at it. Teachers who solely control the evaluative function diminish the capacity for students to participate fully in their learning. The teacher as gatekeeper of information can become a bottleneck for it. When assessment information must pass through the teacher, he or she has to address the assessment needs of 25 or so students per class period. Sharing the essential act of assessment with students increases the number of assessors from one to 26. Sharing the assessment function thus expands the amount of information available for learning.

Much of the value in developing effective students is helping them seek and use assessment information. As students participate in the assessment process, it becomes more efficient. Assessment efficiency, defined as being useful to students, bears no resemblance to efficient scoring. Scoring efficiency refers to the speed and ease of determining a summary score for uses external to the student. From a learning perspective, assessment information is wasted when it bypasses the student in favor of external users. Of course, we cannot make students use information, but it is our obligation to provide it in a way that they can.

Students' participation in assessment is efficient because it allows them to share responsibility for their learning with teachers. When accountability concerns dominate assessment practice, the curriculum becomes obscured in a shroud of secrecy. With the curriculum thus concealed, students experience it in response to teachers. Students' participation in assessment allows them to lift the veil and recognize teachers as resources rather than adversaries. Teachers instruct students to help them gain a clear view of the curriculum and provide assessment information to help them become competent in it. Students benefit by knowing that their teachers did not invent the curriculum but that they can help students learn it.

Lastly, a focus on learning and student involvement in the evaluative process suggests criteria for assessment information that lead to more effective assessment practices. Criteria for judging the value of classroom assessment become the basis for selecting or developing assessment activities and processes. These criteria are described in the next section. The remaining sections of this chapter cover general considerations for effective classroom assessment formats and processes and an overview of assessment procedures in terms of the proposed criteria. This overview does not include the detail necessary to develop specific procedures, but the list of available resources is growing and those seeking information about specific assessment procedures can consult references shown in Appendix B.

Assessment Criteria

General criteria to judge tests include those long used by professionals in educational tests and measurement, fairness, reliability, and validity; the latter two are usually defined in somewhat technical terms. Assessment procedures used in the classroom rarely address technical issues used with commercially developed standardized tests; nevertheless, the importance of consistent (reliable) and accurate (valid) assessment is no less real. Additional criteria are necessary for judging assessments designed for use by students, however. Judgments about classroom assessment call for five criteria: (a) fairness, (b) reliability, (c) validity, (d) the nature and amount of information provided, and (e) contribution to student learning. The traditional testing criteria of fairness, reliability, and validity are defined differently for classroom assessment. Discussion of classroom assessment criteria is enhanced by taking a brief look at traditional perspectives.

Traditional Testing Criteria

Fairness

Regardless of purpose or format, assessments must be fair. Bias is a reasonable antonym for fairness. As commonly used, *bias* often refers to differential treatment of some individuals or groups of individuals, such as those belonging to a particular gender or race.

Reliability

In traditional tests and measurements, reliability refers to the consistency of test results reflected by a quantitative value determined in one of several ways. According to one method, *test-retest reliability,* a reliable assessment is one in which students receive the same score from one assessment to the next. Similarly, *parallel form reliability* is determined by comparing scores on two forms of the same test that are similar but have different specific questions. Yet another definition refers to the extent that results are internally consistent. *Internal consistency reliability* is an indicator of the degree to which a test measures a single dimension, such as spelling or multiplication facts. Commercial test developers report reliability using technical definitions yielding numeric values between zero and one that describe the degree of measurement consistency.

Test reliability has long been important for test developers. In norm-referenced testing, in which the purpose is to discriminate between levels of student performance, test constructors pay close attention to item characteristics, such as their difficulty and test length; tests with items of "medium" difficulty—those that about half the students answer correctly—and tests with more items usually yield more reliable scores than shorter tests or tests consisting of very difficult or very easy items.

Reasons other than test length and item difficulty can also cause test scores to be unreliable, such as the degree of student interest in completing the task. Those who construct assessments external to the classroom recognize multiple sources of variation in test scores and treat them as "error," defined as variation in performance unrelated to what is being measured. Controlling error as much as possible is important for people who test students in absentia. Consequently, sources of test score unreliability receive a lot of attention from those who develop commercial standardized tests. Technical reliability is discussed in terms of scores used for purposes other than to inform learning.

Another type of reliability, referred to as *interrater reliability,* addresses the extent to which two or more raters assign similar scores when rating a performance or a single rater assigns similar scores to the same student performance(s) at different times. The interrater reliability of scoring essays is the subject of much concern and criticism. Teachers are often criticized for their inability to agree with each other or sometimes even themselves about the score of a particular piece of work. Critics do not mention that problems with "subjective" scoring arise in part from the requirement to provide a summary score. Much of the difficulty in achieving reliable performance scores, such as with essays, is the emphasis on holistic scoring. Criticism of the lack of scoring agreement among judges can be extended to all judgmental scoring. The criticism hinges on the prevalent lack of rater agreement in assigning scores to performances that are too complex for scoring as either right or wrong. Some reviewers may judge a paper to be superior, giving it an A, whereas other less impressed reviewers assign it a C. It is also the case that an individual rater may give a different score to the same paper on two different occasions.

Reliability concerns for global ratings of complex tasks point out some of the problems that attend assessment perspectives and purposes beyond the control of the classroom teacher and not directly associated with student learning or competence. Lack of common scoring criteria and standards makes rater agreement difficult; it is also the basis for frustration in students, who approach classroom exercises lacking a clear understanding of what constitutes a complete or adequate performance. Scoring reliability for global or summary scores is far different from reliability for instruction. Helping students learn requires assessment information that is consistent and aligned with instruction and the curriculum.

Validity

Tests themselves are neither valid nor invalid. Validity applies to the *use* of test results. Several validity concepts commonly used include predictive validity, content validity, and face validity. *Predictive validity* refers to the capacity of test scores to estimate future performance based on a test score. Scores of tests such as the ACT or SAT are commonly used to predict the likelihood of success in doing college work. *Content validity* is simply the extent to which a test covers a curriculum objective. Face validity refers to the degree that a test *appears* to reflect the knowledge or skill being assessed. Face validity, often considered the least worthy by test developers, is important for instruction in that assessment tasks should make sense to students. To some extent, this is what "authentic" assessment means.

The use of assessment information is what determines its value for students. Assessment for learning provides students with information that affirms complete performances, describes ways to become competent, or builds confidence; assessment for learning requires criteria different from those used with traditional testing.

Classroom Assessment Criteria

Fairness

As a criterion for effective classroom assessment, fairness encompasses a wider range of issues than simply treating students equally. It also includes ensuring that assessments match the curriculum and are sensitive to the impact they have on students. Above all, fairness means serving all students well. Within the principles offered in Chapter 1, fairness means that everyone has a right to good assessment.

Matching assessments to the curriculum follows from the belief that schools should promote student competence in the curriculum. One often-touted feature of performance assessments is that they match valued performances more closely than other assessment measures do. Well-thought-out assessment activities that address performance are effective, including well-constructed multiple-choice tests that simulate situations and problem settings in ways that match the curriculum.

Assessment that is fair is sensitive to its impact on students. Assessment practices that treat students equally, but poorly, are not "fair." Fairness thus includes ensuring that assessment activities are developmentally appropriate, clearly understood, and provide constructive information in ways that students need and can use. Paradoxically, perhaps, assessment information that is fair is not necessarily the same for all students. The student who is struggling with sentence structure, for example, needs information concerning grammar. Other students may benefit from information and suggestions about other aspects of their writing, such as spelling or argumentation. Fair assessment builds student competence through information that recognizes individual student needs.

Reliability

A common synonym for reliability is consistency. Discussing consistency related to assessment for learning requires that we distinguish between consistent scoring, consistent information, and consistent performances. Tests and measurement professionals place heavy emphasis on the reliability, or consistency, of test scores. The importance of score reliability for measurement professionals is understandable because they use scores in the absence of other information about students tested. These are not the conditions found in classrooms, where teachers have information about the consistency of students' performances.

In the classroom, sources of unreliability take on meaning different from that normally connected with externally developed tests. Assessment for learning requires attention to assessment characteristics, such as climate, and individual characteristics, such as assessment history, discussed in connection with developing effective students. Not only does ongoing assessment in the classroom *allow* teachers to deal with performance variation due to factors (sources of unreliability) other than what the student knows or can do in ways that more sterile testing does not, it is the teachers' professional obligation to do so.

In the classroom, assessment for learning calls for information that describes or affirms performances. Summary scores have limited value in a formative sense, because they provide little specific information about performance. When information about a performance replaces a "score," then consistency applies to the information related to specified criteria, such as correct spelling, complete sentences, identification of requested information, and so forth. Information reliability implies agreement about critical performance criteria between and among raters, including students.

"Errors" in assessing performance occur in the classroom as well as with external testing. As we have seen, a major difference between assessment in the classroom and externally developed tests is that classroom teachers often know what "error" sources contribute to a performance whereas test developers do not. A classification structure for performance variation is useful for classroom assessment. This structure includes four general categories: (a) actual performance or skill; (b) instructions and skill in the assessment setting; (c) individual characteristics such as health, test anxiety, and assessment history; and (d) authentic errors, such as fluctuations of memory or luck.

Performances of skills and facility with content vary. Improving skills and increasing facility in areas such as reading, writing, science, playing a musical instrument, social skills, and so forth are major goals of schooling. Variance between students' performances is irrelevant to the nature and purpose of education or training. Schooling offers opportunities for students to add to their repertoire of skills or improve them. A given skill may be developing or it may be essentially complete, based on defined performance criteria. As has been suggested, one way to define an adequate performance is that it be completed in some way. A completed performance is the learning variable; the outcome of instruction (at least the initial one), the student goal. For classroom assessment, the remaining sources of variation offer clues about differential performance between and within students.

Instructions, Scoring, and Skill in the Test Setting. To successfully complete assessment activities, students need to understand what it is they are to do. Students need to have a "picture" of what the completed performance is to look like or clearly understand the process and mechanics of the activity. Clear instructions about how to complete tasks, including expectations, are important because they affect student performance. Student attempts at a task for which the specifications are not clear can easily result in poor performance. Clear instructions are part of effective assessment, and part of instruction is to ensure that students acquire skills in dealing with a variety of assessment formats.

For writing an essay, for example, it is essential that students understand the nature of the task. Instructions that simply state, "Write an essay about assessment," leave students unclear about how to proceed. Contrast these, from a student perspective, with instructions that say, "Write a 750- to 1,500-word essay that describes an assessment experience you found valuable. Please describe the setting and circumstances of this experience and the criteria you used to determine that it was valuable. Use appropriate punctuation and correct spelling." Again, the example cited earlier about students being told to rewrite a paper deemed inadequate and reread instructions that they find unclear is relevant. Clarity of assigned tasks, including specific criteria about what constitutes a complete performance, is important for students.

Individual Characteristics, Including Health, Assessment Anxiety, Study Skills, and Motivation. Each student comes to the classroom with a unique set of individual characteristics, predispositions, and established performance levels. Some students have severe disabilities that affect their learning and require substantial resources to accommodate them. Students initially enter school with highly varied performance levels or prior learning. Student characteristics often relate directly to assessment, such as their assessment history, and clearly affect learning. Some student characteristics that contribute to variance in performance can be addressed in the school setting, others cannot. Earlier discussion about effective students described individual characteristics that are desirable from an assessment and learning perspective.

Authentic Errors. Authentic errors are a source of variation not limited to students but a part of a general condition of any performance. What constitutes an authentic error varies with the performance involved. Authentic errors include those that occur by chance, such as luck in guessing correct answers. Temporary fluctuations in memory or attention distractions can also cause some variance in performance. Forgetting a period at the end of one or two sentences in the context of an otherwise well-punctuated essay, mismarking a response option, and the omnipresent "typo" are examples of authentic errors.

For classroom assessment, performance reliability refers to the consistency of performance from one assessment activity to the next. In some testing contexts, a major concern about test-retest reliability is students "recalling" answers from previous tests, but for many classroom assessment situations, this issue is moot. In many learning contexts, remembering "answers" from one assessment activity to the next is the point. At the same time, varying the specific content and context of questions is important when the performance requires students to apply their skills to new problems or answer a limited number of questions from a larger domain of important factual material; that is, when the purpose of the test is to address applications, teaching to the test is inappropriate. The meaning attached to sources of unreliability relates to purpose.

Variance in student performance is a concern, particularly when the assessment is infrequent and involves high stakes. It is unfortunate when temporary fatigue, emotional strain, or the assessment setting lead to an uncharacteristically low score for a student. Standardized test developers, sensitive to this issue, encourage test administrators to create the best possible conditions for testing. That students achieve their best is important in these high-stakes settings.

In the classroom assessment environment, too, doing well is clearly important. When assessment information addresses student competence, it is particularly important to acknowledge elements that affect performance. In the classroom, teachers recognize "peak" student performance in the context of "typical" performance; they may be quite different. As teachers well know, variability of student performance is frequent, particularly for some students. Performance variation is of special interest when teaching toward student competence. For example, an atypically well done essay may provide evidence of a student's competence in writing. Students may typically not perform at a high level for reasons other than lack of competence. A poor performance may reflect lack of interest, lack of time to review and rewrite the assignment, or any number of contextual or personal factors. In such cases, portfolios that contain students' best work may better reflect student competence (capacity) than an average score based on a collection of typical work. The student who only occasionally writes an outstanding essay may be a very *competent* writer and feel *confident* in his or her capacity to write well. From a competence perspective, consistency of student performance is not as important as with other assessment purposes.

This is not to suggest that producing consistently good work is not desirable. Developing work habits that include consistency of performance are valued in our culture. From the students' perspective, however, competence and confidence, once established, are theirs. We need to be careful that use of accumulated points as the basis for grades that reflect consistency of performance do not detract from students' competence or their sense of confidence. Assessment for learning focuses on student competence rather than cumulative points. Invalid assessment cannot take competence from students, but it can erode their confidence.

The other side of peak performances are cases in which for a variety of reasons students do not perform well. Teachers often know whether a weak performance is typical or atypical, whether students missed a substantial amount of instruction in a particular area, or whether other factors such as boredom or inattention are present. Instances of performances not representing students' competence, as when they do not constitute a pattern of behavior or when students have a "bad day," represent one source of performance variation. Absent this information, the test score is invalid as a measure of competence. Students who write stellar essays demonstrate their competence; whether they choose to do so consistently is a different issue. Again, a single weak performance may or may not reflect student competence. Although teachers may encourage students to strive for consistent production of high-quality work, they may not need to be concerned about students' competence.

Validity

For classroom assessment, validity refers to building competence and confidence; assessments should be instructionally valid for teachers and students. An emphasis on learning extends the concept of validity to include the process that enables assessment information to contribute to student learning; for present purposes, this is referred to as *process validity.* Process validity is appropriate when the purpose of assessment is to help students see or affirm their progress in the curriculum.

Validity for classroom assessment has a distinctive meaning. Assessment practices that help students develop competence and witness their progress require a definition of validity in terms of the collective set of assessment procedures. Assessment for learning as a dynamic process requires a conception of validity that is also dynamic. The value of assessment information lies in its contribution to student competence. Valid assessment refers to a process rather than specific procedures, because assessment is a means to an end rather than an end in itself.

Assessment as a process is compatible with the belief that teaching and learning predominately rely on formative assessment information. Summative information, often used for purposes external to the student, is also of value for students to confirm their competence or demonstrate it for others. At some point in time, students' competence is affirmed by successful completion of a specific task. But the assessment process assumes performance errors will occur early and require information that constructively addresses those errors. Premature summative assessment, such as grading practice tasks, disallows errors. Mistakes are a natural part of the learning process; assessment for learning avoids a rush to summative judgment.

Nature of Information

The nature and quality of assessment information provided to students determines its value to help them achieve complete performances and competence. Assessment information is routinely used to grade student work, for placement in classes, to instruct students in areas that need improvement, and to confirm or affirm their achievements. Students come to value information in terms of its use or purpose, so communicating assessment information as a grade establishes its value in those terms. Students' attention to summary information about their work, such as percentage correct or B+, too often signals an end to learning and assessment rather than a means to continued assessment and learning.

Information conveyed by assessment activities varies in amount and quality. The content assessed sends a strong message to students about what teachers value. Similarly, the nature of information that teachers (or others) provide students as a result of assessment tasks sends a strong message about what assessment is for. Assessment activities vary widely in the amount of information they convey, from no information at all to specific descriptive statements about competent performances and ways to alter performances

No Information. The least amount of information that a student can receive is no information at all. An example of activities that provide the student with no information is unreviewed homework simply required to be turned in at a specified time. Another example of assessment information not useful for students' learning is national standardized tests. In such cases, specific information about responses that are right or wrong is not (normally) available either to teachers or students. Percentile ranks or stanine scores simply indicate placement of students in comparison with a larger population; they do not inform learning in any specific way. They are useful in providing information regarding individual, class, school, or district performance in comparison with appropriate national norm group performance.

Do Over. The comment to redo a piece of work conveys virtually no information other than the work completed was not satisfactory. Students experience the comment "Do over" as a control issue because it lacks instructional significance; it does not provide the student with a basis for revision or constructively address his or her sense of competence, except perhaps negatively.

Errors Indicated. Identification of errors, such as wrong answers or missed punctuation, provides students with information either about what they do not know or what they did not complete.

Grade. A global reaction to a piece of writing, indicated by a letter grade, informs the student about the general quality of the work or how a specific performance may affect his or her grade. The singular grade may have some meaning in terms of criteria; frequently it does not. The grade B, when it appears alone on a paper, is minimally useful for the student from a learning standpoint. It is adequate information for the student who views school in terms of a grade point average. In a learning environment that emphasizes grades, it can be an adequate professional response.

Percentage Correct. Percentage scores have varied meanings. Percentage correct indicates

1. A sample of a known domain, such as adding two numbers or stating the capital cities of the 50 states
2. A sample of an "unspecified" domain or one consisting of a very large number of instances, such as knowledge about world history
3. The consistency of completing the same task, such as beginning sentences with a capital letter
4. The aggregate of a set of "points" specified in response to a performance task in which points are assigned by groups, for example, 10 points for spelling, 20 points for argumentation, number of instances cited, and so on (multiple criteria)

The varied information reflected in percentage correct has different implications for students. Information that one knows 40 of the 50 state capitals is different from that conveyed by correctly applying the rule to capitalize the first word of sentences 80% of the time. Knowledge of factual information is different from consistency in application of a known rule. Both knowledge and consistency have value, but they mean different things to students in terms of their competence and what they must do to improve it. Improving the consistency of applying a known rule demands more attention to punctuation, whereas "knowing" an additional 10 capitals requires more time to commit them to memory.

Global Comment. A global comment on an essay or other assessment task may give a general indication of the teacher's reaction to the work. Positive global comments, such as "I enjoyed reading your essay" or "Your writing has improved," can provide students a positive overall sense about their effort or affirmation of a competence. Negative global comments, such as "This paper appears to have been hastily prepared" may be occasionally helpful but, because such comments involve high inference, they may result in misinformation for the student. For example, a paper judged as having been "hastily prepared" may have taken a struggling student a significant amount of time.

Negative Comments Only, With Suggestions. Comments, particularly those resulting from "correcting" papers, focus on errors only. Because corrective comments include ideas for change they are usually helpful, especially for secure students. But a steady diet of corrective comments, or too many of them, discourages students and fails to provide affirmation of completed performances or emerging competence.

Negative and Positive Comments, With Suggestions. From a learning perspective, descriptive assessment comments that clearly and constructively provide students with the means for improvement offered in the context of affirming complete performances or emerging competence provide the most complete assessment information. One caution that applies to this complete assessment activity—as well as the preceding activity and others—is providing too much information. Well-intended but copious information can overwhelm students, resulting in their ignoring it.

Time to Use and Timeliness. For assessment information to be effective, students need the chance to use it. Opportunities to use information to revise work, review material, or further develop concepts and skills lead to complete performances and high-quality work. Students should be afforded at least one opportunity to revise their work. Practice tests or activities, trial performances, and writing drafts routinely provide such opportunities. Making information available about performance criteria and standards enhances the value of these activities. In some cases, such practice activities and attendant assessment information help students come to know what the complete performance is.

Assessment formats alone do not ensure that information serves student learning. Rather, the nature and quality of assessment information that students receive along with the opportunity to use it are crucial. Varied use of the multiple choice format illustrates this point. Two teachers, having completed instruction in a particular unit, decide to assess their students' grasp of the material using a multiple-choice test with 20 items. They administer the test under similar conditions. Both teachers score the exams and return them to their students the following day. Students in Class A find a summary grade at the top of their exam expressed as percentage correct and indications of items missed. Their teacher gives students 5 minutes to look over their exams, then collects them and begins to introduce the next unit.

Students in Class B find similar information on their exams, but in this class a review of the test items is undertaken. The teacher notices that everyone missed two items related to a key concept, three students missed nearly all the questions, and all but these three correctly answered at least 15 of the 20 items. The teacher then reviews key concepts related to the two items missed by most of class and the correct solution and common errors associated with each incorrect answer, and schedules time with the three students who missed the majority of items.

The point of this example is that students in these two classes received very different messages about the instruction, assessment, and importance of the tested material. Students in Class A received summary percentage information and indications of missed questions; their test was complete and their scores recorded. Students in Class B were relieved that their teacher assumed responsibility for student "errors" that occurred for everyone in the class. The few students who missed other items knew they were important since time was scheduled for review. The assessment message received by students in these two classes, based on the same test format, was very different.

Contribution to Competence and Confidence

The final criterion for judging assessments is the extent to which they promote student competence and confidence. Achieving competence requires comparisons of performance with criteria and standards. For many skills, achievement is relatively easy to see—for example, catching a ball, tying a shoe, or counting to 10. For other knowledge or skill areas, particularly academic ones, complete performances or competent ones are less readily recognized. In such instances, assessment information is useful to help students see the desired performance. Assessments that are the performance make sensing competence reasonably easy, although not necessarily easily achieved. It is easy to sense the complete performance of riding a bicycle, although it may initially be difficult to do. Making performance criteria explicit for writing exercises is more difficult, but just as necessary. Specifying performance criteria and standards for some tasks is difficult or undesirable. Open-ended tasks with multiple-format options may be constrained by too much specification. In such cases, it is helpful to ask students to simply attempt the task as generally outlined. Information regarding early attempts serves to make the criteria known and help students achieve a complete performance. Additional assessment activities and attendant information contribute to a competent one.

Some students are reluctant to attempt a new and challenging task. Helping them risk a new task requires some measure of safety. My experience is that even graduate students are anxious at the prospect of handing in an initial draft, because they are afraid to expose their perceived ignorance. One way I reassure them is with the reminder that if students can initially complete a high-quality performance without the assistance of feedback, they are in the wrong class. Errors are natural and expected early on in the learning process; the purpose of instruction and assessment is to decrease or eliminate them at the end of the learning process.

Another aspect of assessment information provided in the classroom is the "politics" of assessment. Assessment information, especially when requested, should fit the immediate need or request. Students often seek reassurance (affirmation) rather than information. In general, assessment responses that assure or reassure address confidence, whereas responses that provide information address competence. Using information to promote student competence and confidence is nothing new. The power of assessment information to promote learning has long been recognized, but its value and prevalence in classrooms has diminished due to demands for information that serves external requirements. The challenge educators face is to recognize the power of assessment information and provide it in ways that maximize its usefulness for students.

The politics of assessment speak to its power and impact on students. Some assessment information is relatively neutral; other information is not. We would like to believe that all assessment information is impersonal. Although teachers may act as though they are assessing students' performance rather than assessing students, they must acknowledge that it is difficult for students to separate the two. Students seek competence; assessment information informs them whether they are competent or not. Teachers cannot dodge their responsibility to sensitively assess student performance, because assessment information is effective as received not as given. It is not enough that teachers *intend* to be constructive or helpful, they must also weigh the impact of their statements on students. Establishing an assessment climate that recognizes the power of assessment helps ameliorate its potentially negative attributes. Teachers help students use assessment information by talking about it. Developing effective students includes helping them value assessment information and use it constructively.

Assessment: The Process

Assessment Efficiency: Pace, Haste, and Waste

I earlier discussed reviews of curriculum and instruction, particularly with regard to developing a curriculum that is leaner and instruction that acknowledges goals of varied priority. As assessment for learning naturally follows curriculum and instructional goals, it too should focus on the knowledge and skills that are most critical. Selection of assessment tasks depend on purpose and what they are to accomplish. To address students' factual knowledge or accuracy of solving problems, including complex ones, formats such as multiple-choice or matching or short answer assessment activities are useful. When the interest is in process or skill development, then assessment activities that call forth the desired processes or skills are preferred.

Assessment format, as well as content, impacts the pace of instruction for students. Consider the performance "knowing" the 50 state capitals. An assessment activity to address this performance could be designed in various ways. For example, teachers might ask students to match state capitals with the appropriate state or write the name of the capital next to each state. The method chosen reflects different levels of knowing and requires different amounts of study. Knowing the state capitals by writing them next to each state requires more student effort (memorization) than does recognizing correct capitals from sets of options in a multiple choice format. Assessment formats play a significant role in defining the curriculum as students experience it.

How much testing is needed? How much assessment is needed? The answers depend on the what information is needed for what purpose. For testing, the answer is much less than we now do. Testing done primarily to serve audiences other than students should be held to the minimum that is in students' best interest. For learning, the question is how much of what kind of information students need and can use—how much assessment activity does it take to build and demonstrate competence or understanding? Asking students to demonstrate their competence is legitimate from an instructional point of view because teachers need to assess the effectiveness of their instruction. Beyond this, effective assessment activities are vehicles for *students* to develop and secure their own competence. When the purpose of assessment is student learning, their information requirements dictate the amount of assessment activity needed.

The validity of assessment for learning is tied to the process; information is valid only when it promotes competence and high-quality work. The value of assessment information depends on its being used. Unused assessment information is wasted and therefore inefficient. In this sense, assessment efficiency bears no resemblance to scoring efficiency. We gain assessment efficiency by involving students in the assessment process, limiting the amount of assessment related to student competence previously demonstrated, and considering the ratio of student effort and assessment information.

Student Participation in Assessment

Involving students in the assessment process means that both teachers and students need to have and use assessment information. Teachers help students seek and use assessment information effectively, rather than serve as information gatekeepers. Student participation in the assessment process is a consideration in weighing the amount of assessment needed. Self-assessment and assessment of peers contribute to the amount of assessment information available to students. Helping students become actively involved in the evaluative process adds to both the effectiveness and efficiency of assessment practices. Students are themselves a valuable assessment resource. Providing clear criteria and standards that afford students opportunity to assess and adjust their own performance is efficient. Assessment activities that provide mechanisms for self-assessment, such as flash cards, spell check, answer keys, programmed texts, samples, guides, or checklists involve students in the assessment process.

In my graduate course in classroom assessment, students receive feedback on their class projects from me and from other students. Each student is obligated to consider the feedback and then either make suggested changes or make a case for why changes were not made. This process is valuable, not only because it results in improved work, but because students retain control of the evaluative function and maintain responsibility for their own work. Students' control and personal responsibility for their work free them from blindly following the prescriptions of others.

Homework is an opportunity for students to critically examine their own performance. It allows opportunity to practice routine skills (e.g., flash cards), to improve on a complete performance (e.g., check a paper to ensure that all sentences end with a period), or to pursue an exercise of personal interest that goes beyond required tasks. Student self-assessment as part of homework requires criteria that are explicit and understood. Homework can also be (and frequently is) a negative experience. Working sets of problems without answers provided dilutes the opportunity for students to benefit from their effort and means that the teacher must "check" their papers. Rewriting a paper without guidance or criteria to examine is frustrating and counterproductive. Finally, homework, like work done within the school walls, should encourage high quality. Students who find themselves with 4 hours of assigned work to complete by the next day may choose to skimp on quality or opt out altogether.

Limiting Assessment of Student Competence Previously Demonstrated

Repeated assessment of demonstrated competence is inefficient. For students, redundant assessment of skills in which they are already competent provides little or no useful information. Assessment activities reach a point of diminishing returns. Student worksheets are an example. When using worksheets, assessment questions become, how many long division problems do students need to complete to sense their own competence? At what point does boredom increase errors rather than decrease them? Once affirmed, competent performances belong to students. Assessment of acquired competent performances may be repeated over time, such as review of critical skills and facts or essential safety procedures.

Providing Assessment Information Commensurate With Student Effort

Assessment efficiency improves when the amount of information given matches student effort. Effective teachers use time for assessment judiciously and acknowledge students' time to produce work submitted for review and critique. Demanding tasks or those that require a substantial amount of time to produce deserve more assessment effort than tasks relatively easily completed. The iterative assessment process associated with the development of essays or products using drafts is a good example. In such cases, information is given over time, but not too much at once. Successive approximations to competent performances, beginning with a complete performance, is a useful instructional process, one aided by ongoing assessment information.

As we have seen, from a learning perspective, assessment information is useful only as it is received and used. I earlier defined one quality of effective students as their capacity to seek and use assessment information. A climate that allows students to do so has been recommended. When students fail to use information or follow suggestions, performance does not change. Attending to the assessment climate and process is an effective way to address nonuse of assessment information. Students with limited response to assessment information need help in improving their skill in using it. They may have negative assessment histories and need help recovering from them. Improving students' capacity to give and receive useful assessment information includes making these skills explicit. Students benefit from discussions about the assessment process, its intent, teacher responsibilities, and their responsibilities. Because some students listen and respond up to the point of their responsibilities, we need to remember that as teachers we did not invent geometry, nor can we make students learn it. Once again, we, as teachers, control instruction and assessment; we are commissioned to *provide* useful assessment information, but we cannot *make* students use it. For example, consider the student who, given ideas or specific suggestions to improve an essay needed to change his or her grade, responds, "I like it the way it is."

The teacher carried out the commission to provide constructive information and an opportunity to use it; the student simply chose not to.

Teachers influence the impact of assessment information on students through the process and tools they use. A variety of assessment activities capable of producing assessment information are available. Selecting or developing appropriate assessment tools requires attention to assessment criteria such as the nature and amount information they afford. The ensuing discussion outlines issues to consider when reviewing or developing assessment activities.

Selection and Development of Assessment Activities

It is unproductive to debate which assessment methods are "best" without considering the context, process, and purpose for their use. The critical choice of an assessment method is its appropriateness given a particular purpose or instructional goal. An assessment format may be more or less appropriate than others for certain purposes. "Alternative" assessment methods, such as portfolios and performance assessments, have considerable merit, but multiple choice and short answer formats are neither outdated nor useless. Multiple choice tests can effectively address a variety of curriculum objectives. Multiple choice or short answer tests covering factual material are suitable for some assessment purposes; portfolios or essays better suit others. Each assessment format has its strengths and limitations and appropriate application. Considered use of assessment formats helps teachers address multiple assessment goals that reflect varied instructional goals. The choice of format similarly affects students' perception of the curriculum and their sense of competence. Assessment activities define the curriculum from a student learning perspective; hence, the worth of an activity lies in its capacity to deliver useful information.

To make informed decisions about assessment, it is crucial to ask instructional questions. What do I want students to know or do? How can I determine whether or not students know the important facts in this unit? What level of knowing is desired? Should students supply correct answers or simply recognize them? What might students do that will allow me to assess their capacity to apply skills in novel situations? How can I help students see their progress in writing? What important knowledge or skills appear to require more or better instruction? Which assessment activities deserve much teacher time and effort and which deserve much student time and effort. What information does this assessment activity provide my students? Do my students feel confident in their capacity, for example, to add two-digit numbers? Answers to such questions help connect instructional aims with assessment information. Characteristics of student activities and performances that address instructional aims guide the selection of assessment activities.

Selecting or developing assessment procedures that complement instruction is as important for learning as is deciding on content. Assessment devices and their manner of use in large part govern what students learn and establish students' perception of what is important for them to know. Evidence of the powerful influence assessment has on students' perceptions of what is important for them to learn is the familiar student question, "What will be on the test?" From a learning perspective, the most crucial concern is the use of assessment to promote individual competence. The question that effective students ask becomes, "What will I learn from this assessment activity?" Effective teachers and effective students view assessment as a means to an end rather than an end in itself.

Familiar assessment formats can become more instructionally useful than they currently are through attention to their use. As a specific example, the lack of student opportunity to discuss results and learn from them is a limitation of summative (only) testing. Discussion of results may take too much time or be neglected because of the instructional pace and attendant need to move on to the next unit. Essays returned without comments or suggestions provide students with little in the way of assessment information. Information is a key element for learning; withholding performance information from students curtails learning opportunities. At the same time, a variety of assessment formats can address higher-order skills such as analysis and application and provide productive opportunities to review thinking processes, thereby acting more as an instructional tool than one limited to summative assessment.

The nature and format of assessment activities should suit the skills and knowledge that are valued and assessed. But we need to remember that the assessment activity is not the assessment process. The complete assessment process requires the production and constructive use of information. Constructive assessment, whether formal or informal, is ongoing and matches students' needs and capacity for use. Constructive assessment information need not be withheld simply because the major purpose for the activity is summative. Knowledge of results can be embedded in either formal or informal "tests." Multiple assessment activities may be required to address competence defined by multiple or integrated tasks. Complex and developmental performances often require multiple assessment activities that help students integrate knowledge and skills. Particularly as we move beyond recall of facts, the assessment process becomes more dynamic. Progressive assessment information helps students recognize complete and competent performances.

A steady diet of assessment activities of the same format can bore students. It is not a professional obligation to entertain students, but striving to engage them is. Varied and purposeful assessment activities are as important for promoting student interest as varied instruction. All learning does not necessarily have to be "fun," but instructional and assessment practices that promote rather than deter student interest should be valued. In a similar vein, we need to be aware that copious assessment information can outstrip students' capacity to deal with it. Teaching and learning are intense activities; high-quality experiences are preferred over quantity; breathing room is necessary. Students need occasional breaks from assessment activities, and younger students need frequent breaks.

Assessment Activities

Assessment activities are what students do; in this sense, all assessment is performance assessment. Assessment activities afford students opportunities to expand their knowledge and develop skills, not just demonstrate them. Assessment activities help students recognize knowledge and skills as complete performances and provide a means to acquire competence. Worksheets, flash cards, draft essays, and any activity that provides information are assessment activities. Learning is an active process, so assessment activities must actively engage students. Assessment for learning does not take place only on Friday or at the end of a unit or the close of a semester. Assessment for learning is about students' performances. When developing or choosing assessment activities, we need to decide what information it provides students in terms of their learning.

The informal day-to-day assessment information that teachers provide their students powerfully affects their sense of competence and confidence. Much of what students believe about themselves results from the informal comments of those around them—particularly their teachers. In spite of its prevalence and power, informal assessment receives scant attention in measurement textbooks. An exception to this is found in Peter Airasian's (1994) book, *Classroom Assessment*. In most cases, informal assessment addresses student performance directly and thus provides assessment information that is a means to an end rather than an end in itself. Although informal assessment is routinely formative and constructive, its power to negatively impact students must not be overlooked.

Formal assessment formats that serve as assessment activities include multiple response, short answer, essays, performance assessments, and portfolios. The overview that follows provides comments regarding each format with regard to information productivity and use. The overview focuses on the nature and amount of information that assessments make available for instructional purposes. Descriptive comments also address assessment climate issues and the potential impact on students' views of their competence and confidence, including their level of knowing. This overview focuses on formal assessment procedures but recognizes the critical contribution of informal assessment.

Formal assessments, usually written, are often confused with summative assessment. This should not, and does not have to, be the case. Summative assessment is terminal whereas formal assessment need not be. Formal as well as informal assessment activities are productive for preparing students for summative assessment. In many classroom situations, formative assessment activities are the same as those used for summative purposes. For example, the practice spelling list offered on Monday is the same as the summative version offered on Friday. In this case, the instructional goal is to teach the test. In a process view of assessment, students direct their activities, including self-assessment of spelling attempts, toward a complete or competent performance, however defined. The summative test offers students opportunity to affirm their competence.

Formal Classroom Assessment Activities

In the next several sections, several commonly used formal assessment activities are briefly described in terms of their use, the information they provide, and their timeliness. Several references are available that furnish detailed guidance in developing specific assessment formats; these are listed in Appendix B.

Formal assessment activities, or formats, serve a variety of functions depending on the assessment purpose. Selection of an assessment format depends on the purpose of the activity as well as attributes of the activity. Purposes include assignment of grades, affirmation of student knowledge or performance, diagnostic information about corrective action to be taken by students, affirmation of instruction, and diagnostic information about corrective action to be taken for instruction. Attributes of assessment activities include the nature of information provided; the amount of information provided; criteria, such as recall or recognition; the time required to produce assessment information; and the time required to use assessment information.

As described in the previous chapter, the content assessed sends a strong message to students about what teachers value. Similarly, the nature of information that teachers (or others) provide students as a result of assessment tasks sends a strong message about what assessment is for. Assessment activities vary widely in the amount of information they convey, from no information at all to specific descriptive statements about competent performances and ways to alter performances.

Assessment for learning is a time-consuming process. The production and use of effective assessment information can require substantial effort on the part of teachers or students, or both. When developing or selecting assessment tasks, it is well to consider the effort required and time available for students and teachers as well as the timeliness of information. When assessment is summative, scoring efficiency is valued. When assessment is formative, constructive use by students is the primary criterion. For assessment information to be constructive, students need to use it. Opportunities to use information to revise work, review material, or further develop concepts and skills lead to complete performances and high-quality work. When assessment is formative, students should be afforded opportunities to revise their work, based on constructive criticism. Practice tests, trial performances, essay drafts, and product review routinely provide such opportunities. Making available information about performance criteria and standards enhances the value of these activities. Practice activities along with attendant assessment information help students come to know what a complete or competent performance is.

Several elements that merit consideration in decisions on assessment formats include scoring efficiency, information efficiency, instructional use, the time needed to produce assessment activities and information, and the time needed to use it.

Multiple Response Formats. Multiple response formats require students to select the best response from options that are supplied. The familiar multiple choice test consisting of a question, or stem, and usually between three and five response options, sometimes referred to as foils, is a common variant of this general assessment format. Other commonly used variations of multiple response formats include "true-false" tests and matching exercises; all share the characteristic of asking students to choose, or match, the response that is the best answer to a question or set of questions. Students need only recognize the correct answer rather than supply it. Assessments of this type are often used to assess factual knowledge, although they can be used for higher-order operations and skills. For example, questions can be written that require extended operations to arrive at an answer that matches one of the response options.

Multiple response formats are efficient to score, can cover a wide range of knowledge and skills, and provide broad content coverage. These formats efficiently provide teachers with affirmation of student learning and information for instructional planning, such as early assessment of developed or emerging student knowledge or skills. Multiple response formats can be time consuming to develop, may invite coverage of facts, do not readily provide diagnostic information regarding higher-order skills, and for critical factual material require only recognition as opposed to recall.

Multiple response formats do provide information about what knowledge and skills have been learned—that is, they identify which items students correctly answered and which they did not. Such information is useful to guide individual students' effort and identify instructional strengths and limitations. Typically, this format is of limited use for developing student skills, especially higher-order ones, because of the extended work needed to provide formative information to students. But thoughtfully prepared incorrect response options can provide clues about the nature of student errors and students may be asked to include evidence of the process or procedure used to answer questions.

As is evident from the above discussion, appropriate use of assessment information is the primary criterion for the adequacy of assessment tools. Multiple choice formats may be of limited use as a *learning tool,* when information about the domain is not provided students. Specification of summative assessment tasks should be complete; students need to know what performances will be expected. When a test covers the entire domain it is important that we teach the test. When a test covers only a sample of the domain we need to teach to the test, but not the test itself. Assessment tasks that represent a sample from a large pool of possible operations or factual information, such as computing the mean of 10 numbers or naming the state capitals, are easily modified to provide a different set of items for each test administration, particularly using word processing technology.

From a practical standpoint, the major advantages of multiple choice tests are efficiency and objectivity of scoring. The ease by which these test formats are scored saves time. The objectivity of scoring makes these tests more easily defensible and more apparently "fair" than those that rely on more subjective scoring approaches. Efficient to score, multiple response formats normally provide timely return of assessment information. When items are discussed in terms beyond which are right and which are wrong, students may be able to determine what they need to do to improve their skill. For important factual items, the prescription may simply be that students need time to restudy selected material. Higher-order items suggest a guided process review. When extended formative assessment information will not be shared with students, the multiple response format provides an efficient opportunity for students to demonstrate their knowledge and skills, including higher-order skills.

Short Answer. Short answer tests require a word or brief response to be supplied in response to a set question. In some respects, these are similar to the multiple choice formats except that response options are not provided; students must recall the correct answer rather than simply recognize it. Like multiple response formats, short answer assessment activities provide students with specific information about what they know and what they do not know. Easy to construct and relatively efficient to score, this format is useful for assessing sets of facts that are important enough to demand that students recall them. Because of the added demand of recall versus recognition, short answer formats place heavy emphasis on memorization and thus impact the pace of instruction from students' point of view.

Short answer tests normally allow timely return of assessment information. The prescription for students' use of information is nearly identical to that for multiple choice. Short answer formats may provide evidence of higher-order processes that students used to arrive at answers. When they do, guided review of the process for missed items is called for.

Essay/Free Response. The familiar essay question allows students to construct their own response to a question. The essay provides opportunity to explore not only thinking skills but depth of content knowledge, writing skills, persuasion, knowledge of sequence, concept connections, and creative responses. When considering assessment information associated with essays, it is useful to distinguish between those that call for extended development and those that are produced in a time bound test setting.

Extended essays, such as writing exercises, term papers, or written projects, are typically time consuming for students to produce and for teachers to review or score. As a complex response, essays require specification of often-multiple criteria. As a result, meaningful definition of a complete performance and a competent one can be difficult to communicate to students.

Used as a vehicle for learning, however, an iterative review process serves to describe and clarify complete and competent efforts. Essays developed over time using an iterative review process, including student and peer review of clearly specified but limited criteria, facilitate student use of assessment information. Potentially, reviews of essays provide substantial amounts of information, so much so that periodic reviews based on selected performance criteria may be in students' best interest. From a formative assessment perspective, it is important that the amount of information provided not exceed student capacity or time to use it.

When essays are used in a summative testing context, students do not have opportunity to develop early approximations to the assigned task; therefore specification for the performance needs to be clear and complete. As with other formats, affording students guided practice exercises, including format, help them more effectively respond to essay questions. Another benefit of guided practice for students is that it can ease the task of test scoring. The summative test essay question readily elicits higher-order skills; it is inefficient for assessing factual material other than as needed to create a meaningful response. Clear specification of scoring criteria reduces, but does not eliminate, the subjectivity that attends the scoring of essays.

Performance Assessments. Performance assessments are distinguished by their emphasis on skills or products. These assessment activities require students to "perform," and assessment information, either holistic or analytic, is provided about how well tasks or products meet specified criteria. Like the essay, performance assessment can be applied iteratively and thus help students recognize and achieve complete or competent performances. Potentially rich in information, the value of formative performance assessment lies in the information used by students. When holistically scored only, the value of performance assessment information is diminished, and assessment efficiency is reduced.

Performance assessments can be time consuming, although well-constructed rubrics related to specific performance elements improve efficiency; rubrics expand students' opportunities to participate in the assessment process and thereby contribute to its efficiency. From a learning perspective, the value of rubrics lie in the information they convey. Rubrics that clearly spell out criteria and standards help teachers provide assessment information that is more descriptive than judgmental. Various points or categories associated with well-constructed rubrics differentiate performances by performance characteristics, not simply excellent, good, fair or poor. Thus, rubrics serve to guide learners in their attempts to achieve complete or competent performances.

Portfolios. A substantial amount of formal assessment occurs in the classroom using activities devised or selected by teachers. Formal assessment activities built around instruction provide teachers and students tangible work samples based on explicit criteria that describe complete and competent performances. Portfolios augment the assessment process through reflective and ongoing review of formal assessment activities. Portfolios limited to collections of finished work do not achieve their full potential, although such collections serve students' need to recognize completed and competent performances and teachers' need for information regarding student benchmarks and progress. Portfolios that become simply a folder for all student work are of limited use and easily become unmanageable.

Portfolios are useful for the assessment process, but are not in themselves assessment activities in the same sense as essays, multiple response assessments, or performance assessments. Portfolios are best thought of as vehicles that enhance the assessment process. As part of the process, portfolios serve to promote students' growth and affirm their accomplishments. Portfolios, like other assessment elements, help students use information to recognize their developing competence or become aware of limitations and work to be done. The portfolio provides students with progress anchors and checkpoints and samples of their accomplishments. When "best" work is highlighted, portfolios may offer a more valid indicator of students' competence than summary scores. Students' best efforts show what they can do rather than a summary score that reflects what they typically do.

Assessment Activities: Instructions and Use

Useful characteristics of effective assessment activities are that they be engaging, provide accurate information in a way useful for students, cover important material, and help students recognize complete or competent performances. Clearly, students need to understand the assessment activity, its purpose, and how to go about it and must be provided sufficient time to complete it. The use of a variety of assessment activities helps engage students in the assessment process. Assessment activities used in classrooms should (a) require clear directions and specification of conditions, such as whether reference material can be used; (b) match the purpose and content of instruction; (c) be appropriate in length so as to provide students with a usable amount of information; and (d) provide opportunity for students to receive information and act on it.

Critical to the production and effective use of assessment activities is teacher review and evaluation of their value and use by students. The essential criterion for effective assessment practices is that they promote student learning. We cannot know the extent to which assessment activities are effective until we use them. Assessment for learning is a dynamic process; assessment activities are themselves dynamic and subject to review and revision. At the same time, we need to recall that process validity points to the boundary that limits teachers' responsibility for student learning. Teachers are commissioned to establish assessment practices that provide students either with affirmation of their competence or information on how to achieve it.

Competence in assessment practices is a primary charge of the professional educator. The assessment review process and mechanisms to support it, particularly collegial review, are essential. Teacher-constructed assessments should meet high standards but require a supportive posture as well as professional growth opportunities to develop the skills necessary to create and refine them. Even with assessment training, the process of development requires time and support. Every professional activity and professionally produced product, including assessment activities, must start somewhere; the professional imperative is assessment, a topic to be addressed further in Chapter 5. We begin with the substantial resources we have that include professional teachers, developed lesson plans, and current assessment activities.

Commercial test publishers produce their product using a rigorous process that can span years and relies on substantial efforts of a large number of individuals expert in either process or content. Multiple stages of development, review, revision, field testing, and further revision are a routine part of the process. In spite of the level of effort, reviewers or users often malign tests for their imperfections or limitations. Teachers, who have multiple and ongoing assessment obligations, need support and time to effectively address classroom assessment issues. Effective assessment activities require time to construct and opportunity for their use and review. One consequence of this is that communication of assessment information to students and others needs to take developmental limitations into account. Limitations can be freely explored only when a supportive climate exists.

The dynamic nature of assessment brings us back to the assessment plan discussed in the previous chapter. There, I discussed the value of identifying important curriculum and instruction goals and establishing priorities for them. Now, considering the assessment process, I need to specify more in the plan than instructional goals by planning for effective use of assessment information by teachers and students as well. The complete assessment plan requires full specification of student activities and how to make them useful.

The complete assessment plan includes (a) setting instructional goals, establishing objectives, including priorities, and providing students with representations of complete performances in terms they can understand; (b) instructional activities (lesson plans); (c) assessment activities, such as practice assessments or drafts; (d) information regarding practice sheets or drafts and other student activities, affirming complete performances and offering suggestions for expanded competence; (e) providing time to use assessment information; and (f) examining the impact assessments have on students' view of their knowledge and competence.

The key criterion for assessment activities and the assessment process is the usefulness of information provided to the learner. Assessment information is most useful for students when it

- Provides affirmation of performances or information about what students need to do improve them

- Carries an optimal amount of information
- Is timely and allows students time to use information
- Is sensitive to students (impact)

Information System and Its Use

The emphasis in this book is that the primary purpose of classroom assessment is to promote learning. Learning involves information, provided through instruction and assessment, regarding performance. Effective classrooms are those where assessment information flows freely. Classrooms are conduits for information exchange, directed toward student progress. Effective classrooms require efficient delivery of information students and teachers can use.

The large amount of information associated with effective learning environments place demands on information management. When assessments result in summary scores, the recording of cumulative numeric information is straightforward. When the emphasis is on student competence, recordkeeping requirements change somewhat. Assessment for learning places a premium on information directed toward students.

Portfolios, for example, provide students with evidence of their accomplishments; they are a desirable component of a classroom information system. An emphasis on individual competence and complete performances leads to an information system that features information about students knowledge, skills, and attitudes. From students' and teachers' perspectives, success is the aggregate of completed and competent performances: Examples of completed performances include *students* knowing they can count to 10, read a book, understand multiplication, play the flute, work cooperatively, dribble a basketball, write a letter, recite the state capitals, complete a job application, build a birdhouse, or use a computational formula to solve a problem. Information may be recorded using checklists of complete performances; work samples; competence levels described in terms of criteria and standards, such as accuracy, knowledge, and skills; and reflective statements by students and teachers concerning student performance, student goals, and student needs.

The student information system benefits from both qualitative and quantitative information. It is helpful to distinguish between four meanings of numbers. Numbers vary in the kind of information they represent, a matter of some consequence when we use numbers to convey assessment information. Nominal, or categorical, numbers simply represent two or more categories that are not ordered. So, for example, we might assign a 1 to represent blue eyes, a 2 for green eyes, and so forth. Numbers used in a nominal fashion only represent a particular classification. Ordinal numbers provide a rank-order to attributes. We might assign a 1 to the tallest person in class, a 2 to the next tallest, and so on. A set of ordinal numbers makes no distinction between the size of differences between ranks. Interval and ratio numbers do assume that differences on the continuum have meaning, and in the case of ratio numbers require that zero be meaningful. Numbers having characteristics of ratio scales allow us to make statements such as, "You completed this set of 10 problems in half the time it took you to complete a similar set last week." It is appropriate that teachers consider information conveyed to students in terms of the meaning of "numbers" assigned. Student information may simply assign a category, such as a particular performance is "complete"; imply an order or "progress,"—"Your writing has improved"; or describe a specific degree of change in terms of some attribute, as in the example, "You cut your time to complete this task in half."

A classroom assessment information system aggregates individual student performance information. Teachers control and manage the system and are its primary users because aggregate student performance is a major source of information for monitoring their own performance and provides a substantial part of their professional rewards. The system contains information available from individual student portfolios, journals, or record logs. It may include information about complete performances as well as describe competence in categorical or numeric form.

Parents, administrators, and local administrative boards periodically request student performance information. Within the bounds of confidentiality, students, teachers, and parents access system folders for individual students. Administrative uses of information, such as summary reports to the board of education, normally require only aggregate data. Such aggregated data are likely to contain nominal and descriptive information rather than average values. Information emphases for each audience are

Students—Learning, competence, confidence
Teachers—Instruction and diagnostic feedback (teacher portfolio)
Parents—Descriptive information regarding performances and progress
Administrators/Community/Board of Education—(aggregate competence)

Effective application of assessment practices that promote student competence requires students to acquire new assessment skills. Students need time and experience to find out what assessment information is, how to get it, how to use it effectively, and how to give assessment information to others. They need to recognize high-quality assessment information and to distinguish among its various uses.

Students also need to recognize that learning requires effort in addition to risks. The amount of effort or time expended varies among students. Building and maintaining student effort begins with students experiencing complete performances. The quality of most work will vary among students. It is helpful when teachers avoid perfection and acknowledge authentic errors such as a missed punctuation mark and authentic problems such as illness, stress, or extended work obligations.

Many of the "new" assessment methods being touted have considerable merit; they are worth review by the professional educator. But the assessment process outlined in this chapter—and throughout this book—suggests effective use of assessment information, regardless of method, is a key criterion of the assessment process. Here, I suggest that teachers use any one, or more, of the variety of assessments, depending on what is appropriate for the task. Teachers may need to modify assessment activities as the need arises to better meet instructional needs. Assessment activities cannot be judged independent of their use; the review process, as outlined in the teacher portfolio, is important. This process, including collegial review and active student participation in assessment, when applied over time, can provide opportunities to align staff professionalism with student performance.

5

Assessment: The Professional Imperative

"Professional educators seek to develop and practice their craft to effectively promote student learning."

This chapter is about professional teachers and assessment. It may appear out of place in a book intended to address student assessment, but I include it for three reasons. First, I introduce the teacher assessment portfolio as a means to monitor instruction and assessment. The purpose of the portfolio is to assess the impact of instruction on students, a key point addressed in Chapter 1. The process of judging the effectiveness of instruction and assessment practices is itself assessment. Second, assessment is for everyone and everyone has a right to good assessment. Teachers' personal experience with assessment directed toward professional growth contributes to effective instruction and assessment practices. Teachers also benefit from assessment practices that recognize their autonomy and dignity as professionals. Third, effective assessment practices for students and teachers help initiate and sustain well-deserved personal and professional rewards for effective teaching.

The individually guided process outlined in this chapter acknowledges the substantial talent and effort it takes to teach. It also recognizes that effective teachers and students constitute effective schools. Teachers guide the learning process through their instructional and assessment practices. Classroom teachers, being responsible for instruction in their classrooms, need the authority to practice their profession and increase their professional skills, including proficiency in classroom assessment. To explore changes in assessment practice, teachers need encouragement from colleagues and opportunity to review assessment practice with them. As viewed here, professional growth is a dynamic and individually tailored process but benefits from supportive colleagues. Administrators encourage professional growth when they provide teachers the time and resources necessary to review and alter their practice and when they affirm teachers' work. The belief that professional educators, like other professionals, seek to expand their professional skills undergirds this professional growth perspective. It is likely that the most productive ideas related to classroom assessment mirror the best practices found in classrooms of effective teachers. Identifying and sharing best practices occurs when teachers talk to one another about their craft.

Teachers control assessment practice in their classrooms but are themselves subject to assessments that address certification and professional competence. Guiding previous discussion of student assessment were fundamental assessment principles such as assessment is for everyone, assessment is a process rather than a set of procedures, and everyone has a right to good assessment. I also take the position that assessment is essential for learning—that is, to build competence and instill confidence. These principles, coupled with the premise that teachers seek to expand their professional skills and build confidence in them, suggest that assessment for professional educators and assessment for students share common elements. Professional growth embodies assessment principles congruent with and complementary to effective assessment of students.

Described in this chapter is a professional growth framework grounded in the assessment principles and assessment attributes outlined in Chapter 1. Following the emphasis throughout this book, professional growth means developing teacher competence and confidence that relies on assessment characteristics similar to those earlier proposed for student learning. The assessment process outlined here is not about annual staff evaluations. Nor is it about performance appraisals to award merit pay or determine movement on a career ladder. It is, rather, that professional educators seek to develop and practice their craft to effectively promote student learning. This professional posture encourages reflective practice along with seeking constructive assessment information from others, especially colleagues. The message here is that effective and enduring professional growth occurs as professional teachers examine their practice and build on their strengths through cooperative efforts and collegial exchange. The professional educator views his or her work as a craft and strives to become better at it. Seeking assessment information about effectiveness and ways to improve performance is what characterizes professional teachers; it is what characterizes—or perhaps defines—all professionals (Scriven, 1991).

Supervisory staff assessment practices in education commonly address accountability concerns, occur annually, and are of limited use for improving instructional practice. There is nothing inherently wrong with supervisory assessment of teachers. In the public domain, some accountability is necessary to protect individuals from the rare but serious breaches of professional practice. Contractual, legal, and ethical considerations require administrative mechanisms to support teachers as well as ensure effective public service. But teacher appraisal mechanisms that focus on accountability may offer limited opportunities for professional growth and rarely inspire top individual performance. Checklist reviews of teaching based on brief observations of single teaching segments are a case in point. Teachers who practice their profession in relative isolation and experience "assessment" and attendant feedback only as an annual ritual receive a negative message regarding their work. The following anecdote illustrates the impact perfunctory evaluations can have on staff and the potential value of a more developmental and supportive process.

Several years ago I helped staff at a small midwestern school district evaluate a staff development program designed to be formative, ongoing, and peer based. In the course of that project, I had opportunity to talk with several teachers. What I recall most vividly about that experience is a veteran teacher who, during a personal interview, related to me, "This is the first time in my experience as a teacher that anyone has shown an interest in what I really do in the classroom." This remark reflected her appreciation for the attention and concern that colleagues showed toward her work as a professional and their support of her professional growth. It seems unfortunate that persons in such a critical profession so rarely experience genuine concern for their work.

This anecdote does not reflect a callous disregard for professional growth on the part of administrators but does illustrate the limited time administrators have to address substantive instructional issues, provide useful feedback, or affirm teacher practice. Given the critical work that educators perform, this situation presents a very dismal outlook for education; professional growth is far too important to dismiss because of lack of time. One point of this chapter is that nourishing professional growth need not and should not be the sole responsibility of principals or supervisors. Indeed, encouraging all staff to play an active role in helping each other grow professionally is more effective and efficient than leaving it solely to supervisors.

For the education professional, competence consists of the knowledge and skills necessary to teach. Confidence, on the other hand, follows from successful teaching experiences. Thus, teachers build confidence through accumulated evidence of student learning. Individual and summary student performance information are valuable not only in the professional obligation sense but for teachers' professional well-being. Success, for educators, is the aggregate of individual students' learning, measured one student at a time. Summary information about student performance along with student evaluation of instruction has personal meaning when viewed as part of teachers' professional rewards and growth.

The professional obligation to attend to student performance indicators and student evaluation of instruction can be frightening. A major source for this anxiety comes from those who would place sole responsibility for learning on teachers. External demands for teacher accountability couched in contractual standards of student learning based on standardized test scores is one example of this perspective. This misguided approach is professionally limiting, personally demeaning, and fraught with technical and practical limitations. Willson (1989) discusses reasons why standardized test results are not suitable for evaluating teacher performance. His concerns include the items on the test, the curriculum actually taught, the ability and motivation of the students to learn, the magnitude of the gain in knowledge, and the comparability of the gain with other classes' gains. External demands for teacher accountability through student evaluation of instruction are similarly misguided. Missing in these well-intentioned mandates are minimum standards of student learning to satisfy parents and the community; specification for minimal support, such as class size; and a professional climate. Minimal performance is not what anyone wants, and teachers cannot be held accountable for "personal best."

The professional teacher seeks information about student performance and student perceptions of instruction just as physicians seek information about the "wellness" of their patients and patient perceptions of their bedside manner. Teachers know that fostering student learning is their professional duty and that student perceptions of instruction are valuable to either affirm teaching practices or to change them. But seeking and attending to such information is hindered by student assessment practices themselves, the fear of negative judgments, and the real or perceived lack of safety to take risks.

Student assessment practices can themselves limit the value of student performance data for professional growth. Directives that specify grade distributions or tests designed to ensure a distribution of student performance do a disservice to teachers and students. For example, comparison-based student performance indicators mean that about a third of students achieve "success," a second third receive "acceptable" marks, and the bottom third are "marginal" or "fail." These assessment practices make it difficult for teachers to consider themselves successful for even half of their students.

The belief that teachers are solely responsible for student learning complicates the use of student performance information. As suggested earlier, teachers are responsible for their instruction and assessment practices; they are not, however, solely responsible for the curriculum or student competence. Teachers did not invent geometry; not can they make students learn it. Because students share responsibility for learning, it is professionally advantageous for teachers—and for their charges—to develop effective students. Effective students increase teaching efficiency and add leverage to teachers' professional skills.

Seeking information about our own performance is difficult. Like students, we have assessment histories that include negative judgments of others. Like students, we tend to be anxious about assessment. In a profession as demanding as teaching, anxiety over how we measure up is understandable. The watchdogs, critics, naysayers, disgruntled students, parents, and supervisors all seem to be waiting for us. The paralyzing notion of perfection rivets our attention to secure areas, such as seat time, lesson plans, and following the current prescription for teaching. Teachers, like students, benefit from a safe climate that affords them opportunity to risk assessment. Teachers need to know that their quest for professional growth or affirmation will elicit constructive rather than punitive responses.

Student perceptions of instruction are one invaluable source of information for teachers. But student evaluations, like those of supervisors, may not always be valid or fair. Such evaluations must be disregarded on that basis. For example, if one student submits a negative evaluation in the context of 15 supportive ones, it cannot be the basis for administrative actions damaging to the teacher. Confidentiality of information is important to protect both students and teachers. Opportunities for students to give informal constructive assessment about day-to-day instructional and assessment activities are highly desirable classroom activities that help students participate in their learning. A corrective, external model for performance evaluation and staff development invites teachers' dependence on the judgments of others, making it difficult for them to maintain a professional posture.

Beyond the opportunity to seek assessment of their own teaching, professionalism obligates teachers to promote the professional growth of colleagues. It is a professional obligation to respond to requests for assistance with constructive criticism. Collegial assessment contributes to competence and may promote a general sense of confidence. But meaningful professional confidence for teachers follows only from *personal experience* of successful student learning. This essential point is the cornerstone for professional assessment procedures and becomes the major criterion by which to judge them.

Building teacher competence and confidence through assessment is the focus for this chapter. Many of the ideas presented here follow directly from discussions of assessment-ready students. Characteristics of professional teachers thus include having the expectation to succeed and the capacity to fail, viewing assessment as a means to an end rather than an end in itself, and holding the notion of high-quality work. Later sections describe elements of a professional and collegial assessment process, including criteria by which to judge the their legitimacy and usefulness.

Characteristics of Professional Teachers

The ensuing discussion is not about teachers' facility in assessing students but rather about their readiness to approach assessment in terms of their own professional practice. Professional teachers seek and *use* assessment information to build or maintain their professional skills. Four essential characteristics enable them to use assessment information effectively. Professional teachers seek professional competence and confidence; expect to succeed but have the capacity to fail; view assessment as a means to an end, rather than an end in itself; and recognize the value of high-quality work.

Professional Competence and Confidence

The pursuit of competence is an integral part of being a professional. Professionalism implies activities such as professional training, expanding knowledge about one's content area, and collegial review of practice. These activities share the common quality of contributing to professionals' acquisition and refinement of the knowledge, skills, and attitudes necessary for practicing their craft. Although professional competence entails multiple elements and has many levels, the criterion for effective practice in education is successful completion of teaching performances.

A competent professional performance begins with a complete one. A complete teaching performance includes planning and delivering a complete lesson and *seeking* evidence of student learning. Teaching a complete lesson and *finding* evidence of it being learned is a competent teaching performance, at some minimal level. A competent performance does not mean a perfect one; nor does it depend on the relative performance of others. That a competent performance is independent of the performance of others is important for professional educators since it implies that all teachers can be successful.

Building competence requires information about individual progress toward a performance goal. The culminating assessment, either by personal observation (self-assessment) or the critique of a colleague or mentor, is that the performance has met some adequate level or standard. This standard may be set at any level that includes a complete performance. Thus, for example, a minimum standard for a competent teaching performance may be that at least one student learned one teaching objective as a result of instruction. Clearly, we expect much more from teaching professionals, but a single instance of student learning is the basis for defining teaching effectiveness and professional standards. The aggregate learning of students determines effective teaching. The professional teacher strives for consistency and the capacity to be effective with a variety of students under a variety of conditions.

It is tempting to consider incompetence as the opposite of competence. But it is likely that all, or nearly all, teachers are competent, at least by a minimum standard definition, that is, that one student has learned one teaching objective. The purpose of professional growth—the professional imperative—is to achieve a level of consistency characteristic of professionals. From a professional growth perspective, it is therefore more productive to address professional effectiveness in terms of consistency rather than an arbitrary (and faulty) distinction between competent and incompetent.

Confidence, related to a specific skill or performance, is a step beyond competence. Repeated successful application of a skill or competency leads to confidence; teachers achieve confidence through evidence of effective teaching. Building professional confidence therefore requires information about student learning.

Confidence is critical for teachers' professional well-being and needs to be nourished. Because it is an internal state of being, confidence in oneself cannot be ensured. Affirmations of proficient performances by students and colleagues help build confidence but do not guarantee it. Colleagues or supervisors can express confidence in teachers, but only teachers can experience confidence in themselves. Helping teachers establish and maintain professional confidence is important. Professional confidence is often fragile, particularly for neophyte teachers. Statements that erroneously diminish someone's sense of confidence are grave. This does not, however, justify promoting a false sense of confidence.

The Expectation to Succeed and the Capacity to Fail

Closely related to developing confidence is the professional teachers' expectation to be successful in achieving their instructional goals. This general sense of confidence, including the capacity to attempt new instructional techniques, is a fundamental attribute of effective teachers. Teachers who expect to succeed are professionally optimistic. A general sense of confidence helps individuals attempt professional growth; confidence in specific competencies results from successful teaching. The second of this complementary pair of personal assessment attributes is the capacity to fail. Since failure has severe negative connotations, fear of failure often dictates what individuals are willing to attempt. Yet, being effective in a profession as challenging and demanding as teaching involves multiple attempts, some of which are not successful. Finding that one instructional approach fails, confident teachers look for another one, believing it will be successful. Lacking the expectation to succeed and the capacity to fail, teachers may come to believe either that they cannot teach or that students will not learn; they become professionally paralyzed by the fear of failure. Teacher assessment practices that focus on positive professional growth help reduce the anxiety that attends assessment.

Assessment as a Means to an End Rather Than an End in Itself

One source of assessment anxiety results from teachers' assessment experiences associated with annual performance reviews. In current parlance, the outcomes of such assessments involve "high stakes." In most cases, however, the procedure tends to be perfunctory, predictable, and not associated with professional growth. The annual performance review sends the message that assessment, usually in the form of a satisfactory or passing score, is something to simply endure. Commonly, formal assessment of teachers ends with a completed checklist or rating review that indicates acceptable performance. An acceptable rating does not, however, help teachers conclude they are professionally effective, particularly if it flies in the face of conflicting informal student feedback or student performance information.

Professional growth requires assessment on a more or less continuous basis. When professional assessment is neither an isolated event nor results simply in a "passing" score, it becomes an opportunity to expand professional competence and build confidence. Instances in which teachers experience success based on personally guided assessment—some of the most powerful of all professional experiences—strengthen confidence and serve to establish or strengthen teachers' belief in their capacity as professionals. The timeliness of assessment is important. Teachers who change a lesson plan or use a different instructional strategy or a new assessment method require prompt information about how well it worked.

Assessment information given on an ongoing basis and tied to instruction enables teachers to use assessment. Cast in this light, assessment not only builds skills but also contributes to teachers' recognition of their professional contribution. Information that acknowledges completed performances, such as affirmation by students or colleagues, helps sustain effective and rewarding professional practice. Teaching tasks significant enough to receive attention, support, and ongoing review underscore high-quality work and acknowledge effective teaching.

The Quality of Work

The last of the four characteristics of the professional teacher is recognizing and pursuing work of high quality. For teachers, quality means instruction that leads to student learning; teachers verify effective instructional and assessment practices by students' performances. But since the quality of instructional practices is not solely determined by the degree to which students learn, a cautionary note is in order; student performance measures are a necessary but not sufficient basis on which to judge the quality of teaching. High-quality instruction does not mean that all students necessarily learn but that the reasons some do not learn are due to factors other than deficient instruction.

It is difficult to talk about the quality of work in the absence of criteria and standards. I identified the primary criterion for effective teaching as student performance and suggested that a minimal standard for a competent teaching performance was that at least one student learned something as a result of instruction. Clearly, this is not a professional standard—so what is? The answer to this question is that it depends. It depends on the curriculum (calculus vs. English), instructional topics (some are more difficult than others), student characteristics (their assessment histories, health, and individual backgrounds vary), instructional quality (varies within and between teachers), support quality (such as a class of 15 vs. 30), and the effectiveness of assessment practices (for students and teachers). I offer no quantitative value here, but the answer to the standards question needs to be in terms of student learning and student effort. Providing students with opportunities for learning, including effective assessment information, is a professional duty. Teaching at the level of one's personal best is an individual choice.

Elements of a Professional and Collegial Assessment Process

Teachers benefit from information that affirms their teaching; affirmation is what turns a performance into an accomplishment. Affirmation of teaching helps build professional competence and confidence. Yet, affirmation of teacher performances is infrequent. Teachers working in isolated classrooms miss opportunities to experience the personal rewards of successful teaching and the affirmation of their work by colleagues. When teachers do not routinely gather student comments about instruction, they deny students opportunities to affirm instructional practices and express their appreciation of them. Also, comparison-based student assessment procedures restrict teachers' opportunities to credit themselves for student progress. When we, as teachers, do not seek assessment, we miss opportunities to experience the personal rewards of teaching and the professional affirmation of effective instruction.

An assessment strategy that emphasizes collegial review serves the professional imperative to seek assessment by affirming effective practices and helping to identify instructional practices that need improvement. Such a strategy can include four elements:

- An assessment posture and climate conducive to professional and collegial exchange
- Development of individuals' capacity to seek, receive, and give good criticism
- A focus on student performance
- Promotion of high-quality work

Collegial Assessment Posture and Climate

Review of instructional practices, including assessment, is facilitated through a collegial approach. In this regard, persons expert in instructional or assessment practices render a valuable service, particularly through introducing ideas and building initial skills. But the long-term application and contribution of these ideas depends on the staff who implement them. Collegial sharing of information directed at professional competence is ongoing and demands timely response. This collegial process sustains growth activities and contributes to an effective and healthy work environment. Collegial and professional communication, based on mutual respect and trust, can focus on change or affirmation. At the heart of the professional growth process are the climate and circumstance conducive to collegial interchange, professional growth goals aimed toward improvement rather than perfection, and supportive staff who acknowledge the fundamental dignity and competence of fellow professionals. Isolation and prescription raise barriers to the essential growth process that characterizes professionals.

Effective professional growth begins with a genuine professional attitude toward and between teachers, including recognition and treatment of teachers as professionals. Keys to establishing this posture are assessment practices that encourage teachers to pursue proficiency, seek assessment, and risk change. A key ingredient for professional growth is a work environment that enhances professional communication. Attributes that encourage teachers to seek assessment are confidence and the courage to take professional risks. Teachers' general confidence flourishes when colleagues communicate their belief in them as professionals. A professional climate is important because it enables individuals to accept and benefit from assessment information. Belief in educators communicated by others is especially powerful for instilling confidence in teachers' capacity as professionals. "Teacher-proof" programs, minimum competency tests, and minimum standards corrupt this belief.

Discussions about school climate stress elements related to the overall school environment as it impacts students. The quality of the professional climate is equally important for promoting teacher growth. For teachers to safely seek and use assessment information, they need a sense of professional security. Creating and maintaining a safe and secure assessment climate is part of the professional obligation of school staff. Important assessment climate ingredients include the attributes of assessment introduced in Chapter 1: authority, level of assessment information sought, nature of assessment information, and the emotional charge attached to information. Each has implications for an appropriate professional assessment climate.

Assessment plays a key role in instructional environments; students and teachers commonly experience assessment information as *rewards* for performance. Using assessment information as a reward or for control means that the nature and quality of information are of less importance than its summary value. By way of contrast, less prescriptive teaching styles and assessment procedures free teachers to respond to student needs. Affirmation of teachers' performances derived from colleagues and students helps teachers connect assessment with their personal experience of professional competence. Once beyond minimal accountability requirements, teachers become free to seek meaningful assessment of their professional performance. A professional assessment climate allows teachers to look ahead to their performance and that of their students instead of over their shoulder at prescription and accountability.

The nature of information given teachers in the name of assessment is a critical assessment attribute. As for students, assessment information varies in ways that affect its usefulness; in some cases the character of information dictates its use. Information may be quantitative, such as a number on a Likert scale, or qualitative, as in comments or suggestions. Information may address competence through suggestions for improvement or confidence by affirmation of performance. As the nature of information varies, so too does teachers response to it. Information such as a composite score based on an annual review of a teaching segment may hold little professional meaning. The common tendency for reviewers to attend only to limitations is similarly dysfunctional for professional growth. From a competence perspective, assessment should be specific and relate to teachers' expressed needs. Teachers seek or avoid assessment depending on a variety of factors, including the assessment climate. Because assessment information impacts individuals personally, it may be inappropriate when the timing or character of assessment information does not match the request or situation. Teachers benefit from information that affirms their performance or information about how to change it.

Assessment information that results from annual checklist reviews often emphasizes a particular instructional approach. Generic assessment procedures designed for accountability purposes commonly build on specific instructional elements associated with a particular teaching model. Teachers' attention to these elements can retard their developing their own instructional style. Beginning teachers especially find it difficult to differentiate between comments that reflect stylistic preference versus instructional effectiveness. Persons offering assessment information are obliged to offer information that helps teachers develop or maintain their style. Information intended to improve performance is helpful, but it must take personal style into account.

Emotional charge, the last of the four assessment attributes, describes the emotional force attached to assessment information. Emotional charge affects receipt of information because it emphasizes the personal nature of assessment. The emotional force of a critique, written or oral, by supervisors or peers can profoundly alter its effect on teachers. Individual assessment histories play a significant role in the way teachers experience and react to the emotional charge of information. Recollections of past assessment experiences become the context for current ones. Past experiences that include anxiety and fear limit the potential value of constructive assessment information. Heightened assessment anxiety is especially likely for the beginning probationary teacher.

Although the assessment attributes just discussed control much of teacher reaction to and use of assessment information, the school assessment culture is also important. The general assessment culture includes professional climate elements such as the distribution of information and rewards for performance. Thus, for example, the extent that the school culture is cooperative or competitive is important. Although schools are not inherently competitive, many cultural, institutional, and individual characteristics lead to competition among staff; and competition diminishes collegiality. The contribution of peers to the assessment climate is powerful. Collegial pressure is as great a barrier to individuals' professional growth and well-being as is assessment history. An atmosphere experienced as cooperative helps teachers establish the trust necessary to risk failure and to risk success. Success can be a bigger problem than failure, particularly when the culture is competitive. Elements of a professional community that enhance assessment include mutual trust, confidentiality, openness to questions, shared information, and acceptance of diversity.

Capacity to Seek, Receive, and Give Useful Assessment Information

Critical personal attributes for professional growth are the skills needed to effectively seek and use assessment information *from* peers and to give constructive assessment information *to* peers. It is therefore important that teachers become skilled in using assessment information. Teachers skilled at giving and receiving assessment become valued participants in their peers' professional growth as well as their own. The process of constructive and collegial assessment strengthens professional bonds. Teachers' participation in the assessment process also contributes to their capacity for self-assessment. Self-assessment has several inherent limitations, although some, such as bias, deal with assessment purposes other than professional growth. Nevertheless, it is difficult to judge oneself. Self-assessment is difficult at best, and total reliance on self-assessment is professionally lethal. The value of self-assessment rests on the comparison of valid information with clearly identified goals, criteria, and standards.

Affording teachers opportunities to talk to one another reduces limitations commonly associated with self-assessment. A major impediment to collegial professional growth is teachers working in isolated classrooms. Team teaching and interdisciplinary units are beneficial in that they foster collegial interaction, lead to discussion of student goals and review of pedagogical assumptions, provide opportunities for personal development, and offer professional rewards for cooperative effort. In a cooperative setting, assessment of instruction becomes a habitual process, one that builds on individual teachers' strengths as well as those of the entire staff. Support for instructional decisions based on collective judgment helps teachers establish the confidence necessary for effective instruction and contributes to effective school management. From a school district perspective, collegial assessment can be time efficient. Some of the benefit of team teaching occurs when teachers address assessment issues. The assessment component of shared instructional leadership allows teachers to develop a professional assessment perspective that is qualitatively different from that in isolated classroom settings. The collective development of professional criteria and standards helps teachers soften the personal nature of assessment. In the collegial assessment setting, teachers alternate roles, sometimes giving and sometimes receiving assessment information. Such reciprocity helps teachers frame assessment as professional growth rather than as accountability.

Communities may not adequately recognize the dedication, commitment, and skill of educators, but a majority of parents, students, and community members hold teachers in very high regard. The vast majority of adults remember the teacher who inspired or encouraged them or affirmed a particular strength. As educators, we need to tune in to supportive people who grasp the importance, complexity, and difficulty of good teaching. The naysayers and critics will remain; too often we take our cues from them. Although vocal critics' perspectives provide some basis for self-examination, rarely do their comments constitute good assessment. A major value of parental and community support is to build teachers' confidence, thereby allowing them to accept criticism, either self-directed or offered by others. Such a level of confidence characterizes most programs designed to train individuals for demanding professional performance; too often this is not the case in education.

People vary in capacity to give criticism to others, especially their peers. Many individuals labor under the belief or fear that recipients will take criticism too much to heart, that it will hurt them or result in their distrust. In addition, the knowledge and skill needed to ensure effective and accurate criticism may be lacking. Acquiring knowledge and developing collegial assessment skills, along with appropriate sensitivity to individuals, is a professional obligation. In addition, as reflected by the assessment process outlined here, an assessment climate that provides the necessary context and support for individuals to deal with professional growth issues is needed. We need to talk openly about assessment, its context, and our history with it. We need to define what we seek and ask questions—would you observe my introduction to this unit? How might I strengthen it? Are the instructions for this assessment activity clear?

Focus on Student Performance

The mechanics of teaching matter little if that teaching does not result in student learning. Teacher assessment tied to teaching "correctly" or according to some style rather than teaching "effectively" relegates learning to a secondary position. Evaluation of teachers based on criteria other than instructional outcomes becomes an "add-on" activity. This disparity between the purpose of instruction and the evaluation of it disconnects annual performance evaluations from teachers' professional competence. Teachers' instructional and personal styles represent a mode of practice that "works" for them. Unconventional styles are common in many professions, including sports. Required shifts in styles often force teachers to a mechanistic and sterile approach to instruction and dependence on the prescriptive judgments of others. Such dependence reduces teachers' flexibility and drains their confidence. Instructional criteria that emphasize style over instructional performance limit teachers and student learning. Attention to work effectiveness is a critical characteristic of professionals, and—as is nearly uniformly reported by teachers—a substantial part of teachers' professional satisfaction is *seeing* student progress. An effective professional growth process aligns teacher effectiveness and satisfaction with student learning.

At the same time, student performance measures cause concern among teachers, presumably because they offer a direct link to perceived personal "failure"—what if a student does not learn? Concern about students with whom teachers are not successful is understandable, even laudable, but professionals must temper this concern with what is in students' best interests. This professional obligation carries a potentially high price because linking professional performance with student performance could cause a teacher to leave the teaching profession altogether. School administrators and teachers face a natural tension between serving the community and constructively addressing teachers' professional growth needs. This tension is reflected in two principles: Assessment is for everyone addresses service to the community, and everyone has a right to good assessment means that professionals deserve assessment that is constructive and fair. Professional growth tied to student performance requires an assessment posture that provides collegial support, encourages individual growth, and is clearly fair. Teachers who struggle with personal competence issues deserve more than an announcement that documentation of their limitations has begun.

Given the relationship between teachers' confidence and students' competence, the basis for establishing student performance is important. Basing student performance criteria on norm-referenced measures virtually ensures "failure" for both students and teachers. Similarly, use of performance criteria such as speed or quantity of work instead of complete performances frequently results in perceived instructional failures. Assessment criteria that diminish students' sense of competence also deprive teachers of a rightful sense of instructional effectiveness. Singular standards or expectations disallow a sense of accomplishment based on progress for both students and teachers.

Promoting High-Quality Work

For professional teachers, high-quality work means consistently promoting student learning under a variety of conditions. High-quality teaching is something teachers can recognize but not always achieve. In teaching, however, as in all professions, the pursuit of quality is singularly important. Teachers' pursuit of quality as a professional obligation recognizes that their work is limited by factors beyond their control. The instructional pace, the number of tasks teachers must perform, and conditions in the classroom such as class size and student characteristics all serve to influence the quality of work. A fast instructional pace, frequently associated with emphasis on broad content coverage, leads to instructional assessment criteria such as getting done, completing the text, and so forth. Teachers work in a context that requires accommodation to factors beyond their control. A focus on student learning requires freedom for teachers to pursue quality and support for personal best efforts rather than demands for minimum performances.

Facilities, materials, and equipment also contribute to the quality of work. For teachers to produce high-quality work requires high-quality resources. Lack of equipment, oversized classes, insufficient supplies, or illegible worksheets all send the message that quality is not valued. Teachers and their students routinely surmount limitations in support, but not without cost in learning quality and personal frustration. The efforts of many teachers and their charges who produce high-quality work under adverse circumstances are praiseworthy. Teachers recognize budget limits but agonize over the impact such limits have on their students. Realistic expectations for high-quality support are part of teachers' responsibility to their students.

Teacher Assessment Criteria

Criteria for teacher evaluation imply expectations that impact students as well as teachers. Criteria such as style, content coverage, and instructional pace complicate the delivery of high-quality instruction and use of effective assessment practices. In the process outlined here, high-quality teaching emphasizes complete performances that include evidence of student learning. This perspective involves criteria for teacher assessment that go beyond planning and delivery of "proper" lesson plans to address the impact of instruction. Assessment information that affirms performance or suggests changes to promote student learning differs from information used to certify teachers. Characteristics of such information are described later in this chapter.

Generally agreed on criteria that describe the complete teaching performance help teachers *see* performance elements. For teachers to grow professionally, they need information that describes their performances rather than quantifies it as is common in rating scales. The preference for qualitative information follows from the idea that teaching competence begins with a complete performance. Useful professional assessment involves sharing ideas, tips, shortcuts, and other information that helps teachers achieve effective instructional performances. A complete teaching performance includes gathering evidence about effectiveness by attending to student learning and student reactions to instruction.

Pursuing and maintaining professional competence is a continuous and career-long process. Since there are no guarantees of either the acquisition or the preservation of competence, an aura of tension surrounds professionals as they go about their practice. Regardless of experience, maintaining effective skills and perfecting new skills are continuous challenges for all professionals. Specific needs for professional growth vary from individual to individual; therefore not all teachers need the same staff development offering at the same time. Depending on individual circumstance, some teachers may review and revise their delivery whereas others may alter their assessment practices or change their content focus. Seeking assessment implies a desire to improve professionally; it deserves some measure of professional control.

Plan and Deliver

Planning and delivering instruction is what teachers do. These two essential activities consume most of teachers' professional time. The major personal demand on teachers is to face a classroom of students and deliver instruction. Lesson plans that describe what we do as teachers are necessary to teach and, importantly, provide us with some measure of security. Assessment activities describe what students do. They are clearly important for students. They also are important for teachers because they are the primary means for examining the impact of instructional plans and their delivery. Adding student impact to the planning and delivery process is a key component of a professionally guided assessment process.

As part of the discussion about instructional and assessment blueprints, I introduced the teacher portfolio as a valued instrument for the assessment process. Professionally guided assessment development requires ongoing review and revision. One function of assessment portfolios is to house the documentation needed to review and reflect on assessment information. The portfolio is thus an active document that contains assessment activities, information about using assessments such as their impact on students, considered summaries of student results (where appropriate), and collegial reviews of instruction and assessment activities. I return to the personal professional portfolio here to suggest its value for personally guided professional growth. The information it contains, addressing instruction, assessment, and their combined effectiveness, is a valuable resource and basis for reflective practice.

The way individuals go about their professional growth—the specific focus and complexion of the process—depends on local preference and circumstance. Regardless of specific procedures used, assessment information is needed and a variety of sources are available: (a) student feedback about instruction; (b) student performance information; (c) observation by a chosen peer; (d) personal journals; (e) peer review of instructional products, including tests and other assessment devices; and (f) parent comments.

An effective professional assessment process benefits from information useful for teachers. Characteristics of information based on the assessment framework of this chapter include the amount of assessment information that qualitatively addresses competence and quantitatively addresses confidence, timely assessment that is continuous and ongoing, and clarity of the information from the recipient's perspective.

The Nature and Amount of Assessment Information

Statements made in conjunction with assessment activities vary in the amount and quality of information they convey. In addition, individuals vary in their capacity to receive and use assessment information. One implication of these two premises is that the amount of assessment information has an optimal level for professional growth that depends on individual characteristics and contextual factors. Assessment information given in response to requests can easily become overwhelming. For example, information that suggests changing instructional activities is difficult for a teacher to apply while in the process of teaching. Requests for specific assessment information are helpful to those from whom it is requested. Requests should be based on the amount of information requesters can attend to and use. Specific requests place the requesting teacher in control of the process. Controlling the amount of information respects the effort of providers, as assessment is effective only when used. Requested information also must recognize the providers' qualifications. It would be reasonable to ask students, for example, to respond to the clarity of directions on a performance task but not the task itself.

Qualitative Information. Qualitative assessment information about teacher performance addresses improvement of specific skills. Its focus is competence. Qualitative information is descriptive and addresses specific areas requested by the receiving teacher. Qualitative assessment information affirms performances or points out limitations and provides specific constructive comments within the capability of the provider. The purpose for qualitative assessment information is formative. A collegial review process is most helpful in providing qualitative information, although students also are a useful source. Reflective practice can be helpful within the constraints associated with self-assessment. Performance reviews that offer constructive comments can be informal.

Quantitative Information. Quantitative assessment information addresses consistency. Its focus is confidence. Quantitative information addresses the impact of instruction by aggregating "successful" instructional outcomes in teacher or student performances or in student reactions to instruction. Examples of quantitative performance information include the numbers of students who correctly answer specific questions, achieve a complete performance, or are competent at some performance level. Aggregated student perceptions about instruction, such as their understanding of directions, are another quantitative information source. The purpose of quantitative information is summative. Quantitative information is normally gathered in a formal way but can be obtained informally, such as with a show of hands.

Timely Assessment Information

Professional review of instruction and assessment is a daily or weekly process, not an annual one. Much of teachers' informal assessment occurs during instruction. Teachers routinely seek informal assessment of their instruction, for example, when they ask if students understand the task just assigned. Review of students' individual and collective performances on assessment activities also represents informal assessment of instruction. Such examples illustrate classroom situations in which the usefulness of assessment information is time bound. Students need to understand the task they are about to attempt, and if students' collective performance is lacking, teachers need to decide whether or not to provide additional instruction. Beyond the immediate need, such as clarifying a task for students, information about instruction is useful to alter future practice. Students who ask for clarification of a written assignment need an immediate response; changing the instructions on the assignment improves the activity for its next use.

Team teaching establishes a natural setting for teachers to exchange assessment information in a timely manner. Collegial interaction in such settings includes ongoing observation of instructional practices that offer substantial opportunities to seek collegial assessment. Again, individual teachers must control the conditions for assessment. The positive aspects of these settings can rapidly deteriorate when assessment becomes directed by a self-appointed expert and critic. Another reason for individual control of assessment information is that it can easily become overwhelming. Teachers, as well as students, can meaningfully respond to a limited number of suggestions. As with students, too much information results in waste and frustration.

Clarity of Assessment Information

A critical feature of a professional assessment process is that assessment information be apparent and valid as experienced by the recipient. In qualitative terms, this means that performance features, such as vocal force, are clear to the recipient. Quantitatively, clarity of assessment information refers to the valid aggregation of successful teaching (learning) instances. Effective teachers measure their success one student at a time. Consequently, from a teacher's perspective, it is better to measure instructional consistency using aggregated individual student competence information rather than average change scores. Clarity here refers to the validity of information that directly connects teaching and learning.

Expected benefits of self-directed professional growth include increased teacher autonomy and the elevation of intrinsic professional rewards that lead to increased teacher satisfaction and effectiveness. Over the past 50 or more years, expanded reliance on externally generated student assessment information used for selection coupled with increased teacher dependence on accountability-directed performance evaluations has severed the essential connection between teacher satisfaction and student learning. As a result, students' and teachers' sense of accomplishment that attends competence and effective teaching are diminished. Obsessed with the revelation that performances of students and teachers vary, assessment practices continue to ensure we do not overlook any of them. For some, assessment that does not produce "variance" is simply not assessment. If all students can count to 10, then we need to see how quickly they can do so. If all teachers can teach, then we need an evaluation system that clearly separates individuals with varying levels of expertise.

There are obstacles to implementing a professional approach to professional growth as described here. Contractual limitations, control issues, management emphases, concerns about style, staff competition, and other negative professional climate issues can render this process ineffective. Although many agree that a collegial approach to assessment and professional growth has considerable merit for improving educational practice and making teaching more personally rewarding for educators, it will require courage and commitment to make it happen. Developing and using a professional growth process requires active teacher involvement and administrative support. Providing time for professional growth activities and their effective use head the list of support issues. The personal and professional rewards of self-directed professional growth are well worth the effort, and if we as educators do not engage in professional assessment and the assessment of our instructional programs, someone else will.

Review of Assessment Process and Procedures

Everyone has a right to good assessment. Review of formal appraisal systems and the professional-collegial approach suggested here help build staff confidence in appraisal as a professional activity and recognize its limitations. One source useful for review of either assessment process is the *Standards for the Evaluation of Educational Personnel* (Joint Committee on Standards for Educational Evaluation, 1988). The standards were developed by a national committee made up of representatives from all major national education organizations. They provide a review structure with four categories: propriety, utility, feasibility, and accuracy. These standards were developed primarily for use with formal appraisal systems but are useful for the professional growth process outlined here. As stated in the manual, teachers are encouraged to use the standards

1. To improve their understanding of and skills in personnel evaluation
2. To promote or demand evaluations that lead to increased professional development for themselves and other educators
3. To identify and resolve possible due process issues before mistakes occur in an evaluation
4. To investigate whether given personnel evaluations are fair, valid, practical, and educationally useful

Perhaps no teacher modeling is more important than that encouraging students to seek competence through assessment. Modeling the assessment process described in this chapter allows teachers to make statements to students about their personal knowledge and skill, such as "I don't know, let's find out," and statements about instruction, such as "How can we make this unit more interesting?" A professional growth process driven by teachers' aspiration for increased proficiency and confidence is a model students can emulate while also contributing to teachers' professional well-being.

Adopting this professional assessment perspective can be demanding. Continual attention to student performance and ongoing review of instructional and assessment practices can easily get out of hand. Developing assessment practices in a profession as demanding as teaching takes time. This professional approach promises no quick fix to satisfy the critics of education; nor does it imply immediate transformation of instruction and assessment. The idea of a quickly implemented and easily accomplished remedy for changing classroom practices is as elusive as it is appealing. Teachers, like other professionals, have an obligation to preserve their future capacity, and so should proceed deliberately but at a reasonable pace. Changing classroom practices best occurs through the cooperative effort of professional teachers.

6

Building a Supportive Assessment Culture

"Students and teachers bring life to school buildings; their interactions constitute the school experience; everything else is support."

A perspective about classroom assessment practice began with 10 guiding principles and a reminder that assessments powerfully impact students and professionals alike. I established this assessment perspective by looking *beneath* practices to the beliefs and assumptions on which they are based and *beyond* practices to the impact they have. Assessment for learning is a dynamic process rich in information that occurs over time. Aligning assessment practices with a process view requires more than simply shifting to alternative methods such as portfolios or performance assessments. Although each assessment experience should be useful for students, it is the collective set of assessment experiences that enhance learning. Effective assessment practices build *students'* sense of competence by helping *them* recognize their acquisition of skills or how to improve them. Assessment that serves students rather than others helps them value their own learning and recognize their own competence.

Curriculum and instruction play important roles in assessment practice. Students recognize their competence when they have clear ideas about learning goals and assessment criteria. Meaningful objectives and appropriate criteria, clearly stated, help *students* experience success in terms of competence and recognize their capacity to use skills. Learning experienced as completed tasks coupled with positive assessment experiences favorably impacts all students, not just those who matriculate to 4-year colleges. Positive assessment experiences not only promote competence; they also contribute to the likelihood of continued and lifelong learning.

Effective assessment practices build on substantial resources already in place. In other words, we begin with the students we have, the curriculum and lesson plans we use, and the assessment procedures and experiences already at hand. Reviewing assessment practices in terms of beliefs and goals and attending to their impact on students occurs by topic and assessment activity. Such a review process is necessary because the value of assessment practices cannot be determined short of their being used.

Developing an assessment perspective is far different from implementing one. In addition to examining the beliefs and principles that guide practice, we need to be aware of the context of change, the need for support, and the implications of altering practice and recognize that assessment is itself fundamental to the change process. Both the process and outcomes of adopting a process view of assessment impact schools in significant ways, affecting classroom climate, relationships between students and teachers, relationships between teachers and principals, curriculum, instructional goals, attitudes toward assessment, and the assessment vocabulary we use.

Shifting to alternative assessment strategies without considering basic issues, such as assessment purpose, forces teachers to change their practices without a clear idea of how change will impact them. Similarly, lacking awareness and understanding by students and parents, teachers may find it difficult to create, adapt, and use assessment strategies that depart from current practices.

Examining assessment beliefs, goals, and practices helps us identify the extent that obligations for information other than to the student have come to drive assessment practice. Students, parents, and the community benefit from knowing how assessment purposes and practices impact the learning process. Assessment beliefs and values that acknowledge the power of assessment help familiarize others with the assessment challenges teachers and students face. For example, reducing reliance on assessments that are clearly "objective" and easily defensible from a scoring perspective requires support for reinstating the professional judgment of teachers, reinforced by a collegial posture. Learning objectives that address higher-order thinking skills require assessment activities that foster them. Communicating student progress in terms of complete performances and student competence more descriptively informs parents and others of what students can do. An assessment posture that helps students learn also serves the needs of parents and the community.

The classroom is the basic unit for instruction; a school is a collection of these units. Students experience their classroom in terms of its climate; they experience school in terms of its culture. Teachers establish their classroom climate in the culture of the school. Values and expectations of the prevailing school culture set general parameters that influence classroom climates; a healthy and supportive school culture enhances classroom climates. The focus for this chapter is to move from classroom assessment practices and teachers' responsibility for them to the school assessment culture and attendant support. Supportive school cultures recognize the power and efficiency of an assessment-rich environment for promoting student learning and professional growth.

The perspective throughout this book has been that the purpose of schooling is to promote student competence in the curriculum. Several interdependent elements needed to achieve this purpose formed the focus for chapters describing effective students, a meaningful curriculum, useful assessment information, and a professional staff posture. Throughout, the need for high-quality support and a positive assessment climate have been mentioned. Connections among these elements indicate that learning best occurs when effective students pursue competence in a meaningful curriculum that becomes known to them through useful instruction and assessment practices orchestrated by professional educators. Support for these elements is enhanced though a positive school assessment culture.

From Climate to Culture

I have suggested that individual teachers are responsible for their instruction and assessment practices. I also pointed out limits to their responsibility and thus excluded the curriculum and student competence. Similarly, individual teachers establish and maintain the climate that exists in their classroom, but they do not solely control the school culture. A supportive school culture is important for teachers and for effective assessment practices because it validates teachers' duties and their need to manage them. Assessment for learning, like instruction, occurs in the contexts of individual classrooms and must accommodate their unique needs. A supportive school culture is most helpful when it serves to maintain teachers' personal and professional ownership of instruction and assessment practices. A supportive culture limits the restrictions on teachers' practice, permitting them to exercise their professional obligations in ways that best serve their students. External directives that specify what teachers must do are limiting because they must be at the lowest level that a district is willing to tolerate. Professional obligation takes teachers substantially beyond this minimum level. An effective school culture permits not only professional aspirations but striving for one's personal best as well.

Teachers benefit from a supportive culture and share responsibility for creating it. An effective school culture not only promotes student learning but extends opportunities for professional satisfaction and growth. Mutual support among teachers intensifies professional bonds that lead to affirmation of work and collegial exchange about instructional practices. Five elements distinguish an assessment culture that supports and is supported by effective assessment practices:

- Confidence in teachers as professionals
- A constructive focus

- Effective use of assessment information
- A meaningful curriculum and reasonable duties
- High-quality administrative and materials support

Confidence in Teachers as Professionals

A supportive school culture radiates confidence in people. Teachers discern the confidence others have in them—or lack of it—by the treatment they receive and the comments they hear. As earlier suggested for students, self-confidence expands teachers' capacity to seek assessment of their work. When we believe in teachers, we pay less attention to their "ability" and more attention to their performance. We become less concerned with variability in performances between teachers and more concerned about helping each teacher achieve his or her personal best. Less time is spent deciding whether teachers meet minimum standards and more time helping them exceed such standards.

A Constructive Focus

Supporting teachers in developing their teaching skills and techniques requires assessment that is ongoing. Helping teachers develop confidence requires affirmation of their work. A supportive assessment culture frees teachers to seek assessment regarding their instruction and assessment practices, including affirmation of them. Professional growth, like learning, involves risk. Asking a colleague to observe and critique an instructional unit or review and comment on an assessment activity exposes one's professional self. To take such a risk, a teacher must feel a measure of safety. Contributing to a safe assessment culture for colleagues is a professional obligation, one that implies reciprocity.

An effective assessment culture emphasizes the constructive use of assessment but recognizes its power to wound. Assessment of colleagues acknowledges critical attributes assessment information. Teachers, like students, experience assessment in light of their unique assessment histories. A part of the professional growth process is to help colleagues overcome histories that limit their capacity to seek and use the advice of others. Thus, an effective assessment culture is one in which the personal and emotional nature of assessment is discussed.

Seeking assessment information from students also entails risks for teachers and their students. The prospect that some students may relate negative information is frightening for teachers. It is therefore important that we ask students to describe instructional and assessment practices, not judge them. For students, there is a reciprocal safety issue. Candid and useful information is most likely when students know their comments will not influence their grade or be used to penalize them. Procedures used to gather assessment information must ensure anonymity and individual safety for both teachers and students. Once again, a supportive assessment climate contributes to constructive, not punitive, use of assessment information. Pursuit of effective assessment information from students requires that they are aware of the purpose of assessment information and are instructed in giving it constructively.

A professional and supportive assessment culture acknowledges the tension that exists between professional responsibility and personal accountability. According to *Merriam Webster's Collegiate Dictionary*, *responsibility* is to hold a duty or (public) trust whereas *accountability* suggests the imminence of retribution for an unfulfilled trust or violated obligation. Responsibility, then, is held by individuals, whereas accountability is imposed externally. Responsibility implies trust; accountability suggests reprisal. Professional teachers assume responsibility for instruction and assessment that promote learning, but they are not solely accountable for student learning. Effective assessment practices, for example, suggest that teachers ensure that students have opportunities to use assessment information to alter their performance. Teachers cannot, however, be held accountable if students do not avail themselves of the opportunities to use the information teachers provide. From a professional perspective, a work environment that emphasizes accountability is limiting because it directs attention toward the imminence of retribution. From a student learning perspective, a focus on accountability is limiting because it demands that teachers be accountable to audiences other than their students. Finally, personal best cannot be a system demand or requirement. Personal best follows from teachers' concern for professional rewards tied to student progress and performance. Personal best derives from individuals wanting to be professionally competent. Effective assessment cultures help teachers realize professional rewards through collegial support and attention to student learning.

Seeking assessment is an effective way to disarm the accountability critics, legitimately so when criticism involves the teachers' professional prerogatives, instruction, and assessment. Seeking assessment helps teachers maintain personal control over their practices. The individually guided assessment review process suggested here permits teachers to exercise the evaluative function that is similarly so essential for effective students. I earlier mentioned the importance of students using assessment information for their learning; teachers similarly benefit from reflective practice that includes their use of information.

Effective Use of Assessment Information

Effective and efficient use of assessment information requires teachers to talk with one another: If we want to develop positive learning attitudes, camaraderie and cooperation among staff and students is needed. A professional obligation of teachers is to help one another, and the school culture can either enhance or diminish opportunities to do so. Team teaching, for example, is more than several teachers presenting a class together; it affords opportunity for true collegial practice.

When considering effective use of assessment information, it is helpful to acknowledge that teachers' performances vary. Collegial practice helps all teachers examine the impact of their practices. An assessment posture is needed that provides information teachers can use to develop or affirm their skills and build their confidence. Effective use of assessment information is efficient. For example, it is inefficient for professional teachers to use precious time to review practices and skills in which they are already competent or confident, except to reaffirm competence or build confidence. Professional growth focused on a limited number of elements enhances assessment efficiency and ensures time for assessment information use. Other elements that improve efficiency are the use of meaningful criteria for assessment information; the use of a variety of assessors, including colleagues and students; and the development of staff and student capacity to give constructive assessment information.

A Meaningful Curriculum and Reasonable Duties

A supportive work culture acknowledges the relationship between the quality of work and the pace of instruction. Serious curriculum review requires examination of content and what can be meaningfully taught. It is reasonable for teachers to expect that the curriculum reflect valid content and criteria and that teachers have adequate time to present the curriculum and provide useful assessment information for students. It is in students' best interests that teachers have reasonable duties that allow them to focus on instruction and student learning.

High-Quality Support

Closely related to meaningful curriculum and reasonable duties is the quality of material and administrative support of teachers. If teachers and students are to succeed, they need a work environment that includes reasonable class sizes, equipment that works, handouts that are legible, a place to work, technology support, and so forth. It is contradictory to expect quality work from teachers or students in the absence of quality support. It is troublesome for teachers to challenge students to do high-quality work if the assessment activity they receive is not legible. The job of developing effective lesson plans and assessment activities requires ongoing review and revision; such work becomes arduous without technology such as word processing and ready access to high-quality printing support. If teachers are to have collegial discussions about their craft, they need the time and a place to do so.

Teachers have long been noted for their capacity to deal with limited resources; they know textbooks are expensive, paper is in short supply, and

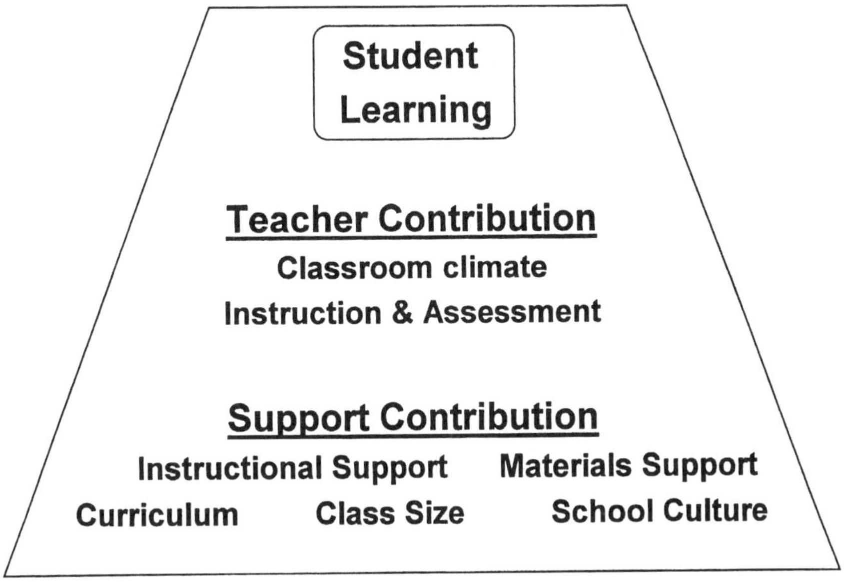

Figure 6.1. Contributions to Student Learning

many aging school buildings offer limited amenities. Material and administrative support comes from budgets that have limits. Limited resources have always been a part of public education and that history likely will continue. The challenge is to weigh the impact material support has on instruction as well as to consider ways to make it efficient. Emphasis on quality over quantity applies to support as well as curriculum. These become reasonable expectations for teachers—these are things they should seek. The challenge for school districts is to promote these characteristics. Teachers develop and maintain their classroom climates, but only in the context of the prevailing school culture.

Effective instruction and assessment practices are the essential elements of learning for which teachers are responsible. But teachers operate in a context of accommodation. Multiple obstacles to optimal learning for all students exist over which teachers have little or no control. Students, teachers, administrative and support staff, parents, and the community all contribute to student learning. Support elements that help translate the curriculum to competent students, through instruction and assessment, are shown in Figure 6.1.

Local Review

The review and development of local assessment cultures can be accomplished in a variety of ways, and whether they are school based or district based, formal or informal, is not important. It is important, however, that the process go beyond simple review of test formats and procedures. Developing supportive assessment cultures, like developing effective classroom assessment climates, means looking beneath practices to beliefs and beyond practices to their impact on people. Taking advantage of the constructive power of assessment means looking at the way it is used. The general strategy outlined in Chapter 1 can help individuals, school staff, and communities address the questions they need to answer. Questions that help frame the process and stimulate discussion about critical assessment components include:

1. How does assessment serve learning?
2. Are assessment beliefs, goals, and practices aligned?
3. How is assessment information used by students, district staff, parents, and others?
4. How is information reported? What does it mean?
5. What impact does information have on students' learning?

Reviewing assessment practices requires that teachers use assessment information. Effective assessment practices begin with what is already in place. School districts have professional staff, effective students, and support elements in place. The review process will likely affirm many practices and suggest change in others. Changing practices will require widespread support. For example, to reinstitute professional judgment of teachers as an acceptable practice a support system for dealing with questioned assessments will have to be in place, reinforced by a collegial posture among teachers and a supportive posture by parents and the community. Cautions for this review are that change should occur deliberately, but at a pace that allows high quality.

The fundamentals of assessment talked about here serve as building blocks both for improving practice and expanding knowledge about assessment. Classroom teachers have the opportunity not only to explore and develop assessment strategies in a way that can change their practice but also to help shape assessment practice itself.

Community Culture

Schools operate in the culture of their community; community support is thus vital to the life and culture of the school. At appropriate times as school districts or individual schools review and change assessment strategies, it will be helpful to involve parents and to inform the larger community. Every parent and community member has a stake in education, either in the long or short term; their involvement in decisions, or at least ensuring that they have opportunity for meaningful involvement, is important if their support is to be realized. In many cases, parents and the larger community simply want to be informed or have opportunity to become informed about their schools.

Schools and communities can benefit from developing a clear sense of what they want their students to know and be like; each needs to decide. Although it is difficult to establish curriculum goals because of varied and sometimes conflicting opinions of community members, school staff, parents, and students, it is nevertheless critically important. Teachers benefit from a clearly specified and meaningful curriculum. Students need to know what is important, what will be reviewed, and what will be assessed. One-shot assessment limits student control, diminishes the importance of knowledge and skills, inhibits learning, ignores competence, and does not develop student perseverance and patience.

Educators are rightfully concerned about balancing their professional prerogatives with parental and community input. It is in the interest of students that teachers exercise control over their professional practice. Holding open forums on professional issues promotes parent and community awareness concerning important issues but may invite controversy. Community members and parents may not appreciate the challenges and obstacles that face teachers, but we should not forget that most of them hold teachers in high regard. The potential value of community support resulting from open discussions of substantive issues likely outweighs the potential for controversy. Business, civic, and parent-teacher organizations can affirm their communities' schools as well as provide valuable insights.

Concluding Statements

This book is about people and assessment—professional teachers and effective students. This book could have been written for student assessment only, but I believe such an approach misses the point. Assessment is a process, an attitude. Assessment is for everyone, staff and students alike. Staff, students, and the community benefit from a culture that promotes learning; such a culture helps everyone experience a healthy education system by engaging them in a learning process directed at personal progress and competence. Our task is to increase the amount of assessment information that promotes learning. We do this most efficiently by helping colleagues become more effective teachers and helping students become more effective learners. The focus is on improvement; competence is the goal; assessment is the means; we begin with a complete performance.

Change is not easy. Tradition, personal experience, and comfort with current practice all act to discourage change. The positive aspect of the framework described here is that the change process is based on ongoing assessment. Only after assessment principles, beliefs, and goals are established, do we know the criteria for judging the effectiveness and efficiency of assessment practices. Only when the impact of assessment practices is considered can we judge their adequacy for promoting student learning. Thus, effective assessment practices are not tests simply planned and used; they are dynamic activities that evolve based on their value for students and teachers.

Every student eventually faces selection decisions and communities have a right to some measure of accountability. Apart from this, schools are about learning and assessment should serve learning. But no matter how hard we try to avoid them, comparisons of our performances with those of others occur. Students on every playground know who can run the fastest, who they perceive to be the "smartest"; every parent worries whether Mary or John measures up to their peers; and community members are concerned about how their schools compare with those of neighboring communities. But if accountability and selection concerns dominate assessment issues, learning and quality are diminished. When external requirements oblige the support of the school community at the expense of student learning, the system is out of balance. Students and their teachers bring life to school buildings; their interactions constitute the school experience; everything else is support.

National standards may provide some useful benchmarks for local schools. Although national standards represent one approach for improving education, I believe we will develop better schools by relying on the talent and support of local staff, students, and the community. History reminds us that an accountability posture limits human productivity; it is unlikely that we will achieve a world-class education system using an accountability model.

Effective school cultures promote the personal best of their members. Effective school cultures gather energy from the collective pursuit of personal progress and competence rather than expend energy on individual competition for awards. Effective school cultures show more interest in personal best than who is best and more concern with expanding individual opportunity than limiting it. Finally, effective school cultures find direction in clearly articulated principles and strength in the constructive value of assessment information.

Increasingly, especially since World War II, successful students have been defined in somewhat singular terms, notably by their being admitted to or selected for a college program, perhaps even a prestigious one. We hear a lot about the high-stakes assessments that contribute to such decisions and impact students in significant ways. But in the long run, assessments for truly high stakes are those that students experience on a daily basis in the classroom over the duration of their education experience. Effective classroom instruction and assessment are the primary means by which students accumulate the knowledge, skills, and attitudes needed for them to become contributing members of society. Assessment practices that encourage high-quality work and affirm unique student attributes represent a return to the educational heritage on which the United States was founded, namely, education for an informed citizenry, education to build individual competence and know-how; with such an emphasis schools help *all* students become productive adults.

Chapter Activities

The activities and questions to address described in the following six sections are offered to help you understand and apply the ideas in this book to your professional practice. The section headings correspond to the book's six chapters. Some activities and questions have parallel components in the personal professional portfolio outlined in Appendix A. You are invited to use your portfolio to record your responses to selected or all of questions and activities found in these sections.

Chapter 1: Assessment Foundations: Beliefs

Reflect on your personal experiences with assessment, both positive and negative. Identify the conditions or characteristics that made them impact you positively or negatively.

List your beliefs and assumptions about learning, students, and assessment: You might begin by stating or restating those beliefs you agree with that were offered in Chapter 1.

Discuss your assessment beliefs and goals with a colleague(s) or in a study group.

List assessment practices you experienced as a student. List assessment practices you commonly use as a teacher. How are they different? How are they the same?

Consider your assessment practices in terms of six assessment attributes described in Chapter 1:

1. Are students active participants in learning and assessment activities?

2. What kind of assessment information do your students seek?
3. Consider the nature and amount of assessment information you give students. Do your students typically use assessment information? How do they use it?
4. How much opportunity do your students have to use assessment information?
5. What emotional charge do you attach to the assessment information you give?
6. What aspects of your assessment setting or climate contribute to students seeking and using assessment information?

What do the 10 assessment beliefs and 6 assessment attributes suggest for your assessment goals and practices?

How closely do your current assessment practices match your assessment goals and beliefs?

Consider the power of assessment. What does the phrase "Instruction touches the mind, assessment touches the heart" mean to you?

Chapter 2: Developing Effective Students

Reflect on assessment practices in a climate that encourages risk taking. Answer the following questions based on your assessment practices.

1. Do I call only on students who volunteer to answer?	Yes ____	No ____
2. Do I encourage students to risk answering questions even if they are unsure of their answer?	Yes____	No ____
3. Do I point out errors in student responses in a positive fashion?	Yes ____	No ____
4. Do I talk with students about the constructive value of assessment information?	Yes ____	No ____
5. Do I help students discover how to use assessment information from others and to develop skills in assessing their own work?	Yes ____	No ____
6. Do I encourage students to seek assessment information?	Yes ____	No ____
7. Do I help students establish confidence as learners?	Yes ____	No ____
8. Do I let students know that I appreciate their work?	Yes ____	No ____
9. Do I affirm students' efforts as well as their performance?	Yes ____	No ____
10. Do I help students recognize complete performances and levels of competence? Are performance criteria and standards clear?	Yes ____	No ____

11. Do I help students experience the curriculum in meaningful ways? Yes ____ No ____
12. Do I provide practice exercises? Yes ____ No ____
13. Do I monitor the impact of assessment information and the quality of the assessment climate? Yes ____ No ____

For items you answered no, consider how you might alter your assessment practices or what barriers need to be addressed to allow you to alter your practices.

Monitor the impacts your assessment practices have on students:

1. Ask students to tell you what assessment information is useful to them.
2. Ask students to react to the amount of information; is it too much or too little?
3. Look for evidence that assessment information has been used.
4. Affirm students' use of assessment information to improve their performance.

Chapter 3: A Manageable Curriculum

Think about the curriculum you teach, the pace of your instruction, its impact on students, and the quality of their work. You might begin by reviewing the time you currently spend on selected topics or units.

For a selected unit, topic, or lesson, describe and prioritize the instructional aims and objectives. Establish performance criteria and standards for each instructional aim.

Sample General Assessment Criteria

Level of knowing: Recognize, recall, find
Speed
Consistency (apply a known rule)
Correct process
Spelling and grammar
Time
Length
Correct answers
Creativity
Legibility

---

1. Do the aims and criteria describe a complete performance? Yes ____ No ____

2. Which instructional goals and objectives are most important? (See state capitals example in Appendix D)	Yes ____	No ____
3. Is this unit or topic defined such that student learnings or performances can be clearly defined?	Yes ____	No ____
4. Are instructional objectives combined to form complete performances that are meaningful for students?	Yes ____	No ____
5. Are all the learning objectives needed for this unit?	Yes ____	No ____
6. Are the objectives at an appropriate level for my students?	Yes ____	No ____
7. Do student performance criteria reflect my instructional priorities?	Yes ____	No ____
8. Do the performance criteria and standards define complete or competent performances?	Yes ____	No ____

For items you answered no, consider how you might alter your assessment practices or what barriers need to be addressed to allow you to alter your practices.

For one or more of your instructional aims, determine whether competent performances are more than, less than, or the same as complete performances (refer to Table 3.1 in Chapter 3).

Chapter 4: Using Assessment Information Effectively

Create an assessment plan beginning with your current assessment practices and process. The assessment plan may be an integral part of your lesson plan or referenced to it. The assessment plan begins with instructional aims defined in terms of complete performances. Use the instructional aim(s) for a lesson or unit in complete performance terms addressed in Chapter 3.

Review existing assessment activities or create new ones that will help students achieve complete or competent performances that coincide with your instructional aims. Remember that assessment activities are vehicles to help students engage the curriculum and receive affirmation or information about their performances.

Identify sources and types of information that are available for students:

Teacher review of drafts or products
Self or peer review
Assessment guides that apply to the performance such as answer keys
Checklists, flash cards, computer software
Programmed texts

Review or establish conditions that encourage use of assessment information by attending to assessment attributes (see Chapter 1).

Review general assessment activity conditions:

Open book/closed book
Use of computational devices (yes/no)
Work done independently or cooperatively
Open or constrained format
Typed versus handwritten
Work completed in class or at home

Review general assessment activity format:

Legible
Clear instructions
Engaging (style/flair)
Spelling/punctuation
Sources of assessment information specified (Teacher, Peers, Student, Key, Checklist)

Monitor the instruction and assessment process in terms of

The pace of instruction
Usefulness of assessment information
Aggregate student information:
 Performance summaries
 Reactions to instruction, such as pace and assessment activities

Review and revise specific assessment activities, one at a time.

Separate performance-referenced (formative) and grade-referenced (summative) assessment tasks. The learning process involves errors and requires opportunity for students to use assessment information to improve their performances. If grades are used, align them with performance as closely as possible and provide students opportunities to prepare for summative tasks (see Appendix C).

Establish a process for review by answering a series of questions regarding curriculum, instruction and assessment. These include

Can performances be reliably reviewed?
Are instructions for assessment activities clear in terms of students knowing what they are to do?
Are the criteria and standards for assessment clearly defined, for example, all sentences have a period, begin with a capital letter, and so forth.
How much time does the assessment activity require for students and for you?

How many exemplars are needed to demonstrate proficiency or understanding?

Impact of Assessment Practices

Monitor instances of students seeking assessment.

Look for evidence of use of information by students, such as revisions to products or performances.

Consider a process review to include assessment attributes such as the nature of information provided and the opportunity/time to use it.

---

1. Does the assessment information I give match that which is sought? Yes ____ No ____
2. Is the nature and amount of assessment information useful for students? Yes ____ No ____
3. Do I provide adequate time for students to use assessment information? Yes ____ No ____
4. Does the emotional charge I attach to assessment information hinder students' use of it? Yes ____ No ____
5. Is the classroom climate conducive to students seeking assessment information? Yes ____ No ____

Chapter 5: Assessment: The Professional Imperative

Begin and maintain a personal professional portfolio (see Appendix A).

Define your professional goals.

List your personal strengths and limitations.

When was the last time you sought out assessment information from a colleague?

What keeps you from seeking assessment information from others (colleagues, students)?

Consider your collegial assessment skills and techniques in terms of the assessment attributes presented in Chapter 1.

Consider ways to strengthen your capacity to give and receive constructive assessment information.

Seek out a trusted colleague and talk about a collegial assessment process. Request specific information, such as asking if he or she would be willing to review a teaching segment or comment on an assessment activity.

Look for personal professional rewards in terms of student growth (increased competence).

Attend to students' reactions to assessment information.

Reflect on the limits of your teaching responsibility in terms of instruction and assessment.

Seek professional training experiences as they might benefit you.

How do professional colleagues support my efforts to improve my teaching?

How much time do I have to pursue professional growth activities?

What changes in the professional climate in my school would help me risk new instruction and assessment strategies?

How do performance appraisals enhance my effectiveness as a teacher?

How does the school climate affect my assessment practices?

How do student and parent expectations affect my assessment practices?

Discuss with colleagues ways to establish a supportive professional school culture that encourages sharing constructive assessment information and reflective practice.

Appendix A: Personal Professional Portfolio

The purpose of the personal portfolio is to help you seek and use constructive assessment information to build professional skills and secure personal professional rewards. This professional portfolio is intended to serve you. It should be confidential and not used for district appraisal, except as you choose. The personal portfolio is a vehicle to record, monitor, and refine your professional practices, including those related to assessment. Seeking information about one's own performance is professionally valuable but involves personal risk. You can and should determine the risks you are willing to take. It is vital that personal professional risks take place in a safe and supportive work culture. It will be advantageous for you to exercise some control over the nature and amount of information you receive. Information that is descriptive rather than judgmental is preferred. It is appropriate that you seek affirmation of your instruction and assessment skills as well as suggestions that might strengthen them.

Major portfolio components include your lesson plans and assessment plans, student performance information, student reactions to instruction and assessment, and comments from colleagues (see Figure A.1). At the heart of the portfolio is a personal journal. Journal entries allow you to reflect on your instruction and assessment practices and take advantage of constructive assessment information from others.

Topics to consider for your portfolio and journal are listed below as a general guide; altering them to suit your needs and style is encouraged.

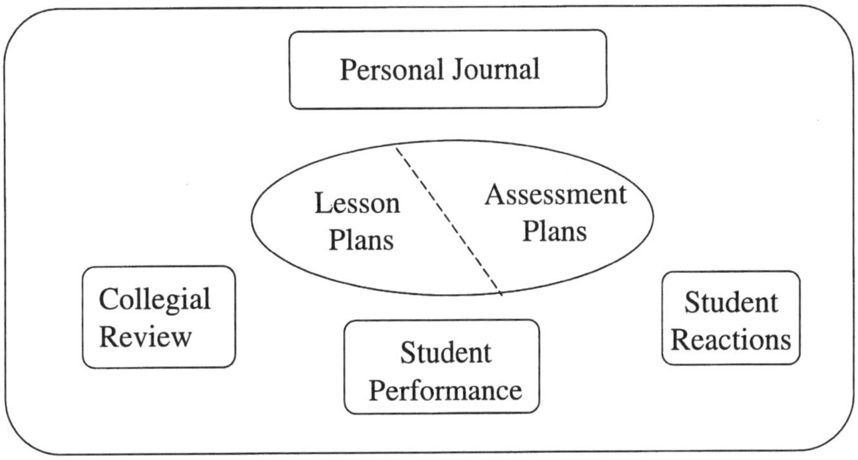

Figure A.1.

I. Personal Assessment Experiences

Positive:

Negative:

Reflections:

My assessment beliefs:

1.
2.
3.

Consider the power of assessment: "Instruction touches the mind; assessment touches the heart." What does this phrase mean to me?

Personal journal entries might include information and reflections regarding

- Effective students:
  - Student performance summaries
  - Student reactions to instruction and assessment
- Meaningful curriculum:
  - Pace of instruction
  - Quality of work
- Use of assessment information by students:
  - Five assessment attributes
  - Assessment climate (e.g., do my students ask questions, seek assessment information, feel comfortable offering answers in class?)

Professional rewards such as evidence of student effort, growth, and competence in valued learnings

II. Assessment Information From Others

Collegial review:
- Observation of instruction
- Review of assessment process or activities
- Review of classroom assessment climate
- Discussion of school assessment culture

Student reactions to instruction and assessment:
- Casual student comments regarding instruction or assessment
- Evidence of student engagement in instruction and assessment activities
- Student performance summaries (by class)
- Units/topics/performances students performed well
- Units/topics/performance that appear to be not well understood

Appendix B: Suggested Readings

Airasian, Peter W. 1994. *Classroom Assessment* (2nd ed.). New York: McGraw-Hill.

Joint Committee on Standards for Educational Evaluation, Daniel L. Stufflebeam, Chair. 1988. *Standards for the Evaluation of Educational Personnel.* Newbury Park, CA: Sage.

Linn, Robert L., and Gronlund, Norman E. 1995. *Measurement and Assessment in Teaching* (7th ed.). Englewood Cliffs, NJ: Merrill.

Popham, W. James. 1995. *Classroom Assessment: What Teachers Need to Know.* Boston: Allyn & Bacon.

Stiggins, Richard J. 1994. *Student-Centered Classroom Assessment.* New York: Merrill.

Wiggins, Grant P. 1993. *Assessing Student Performance.* San Francisco: Jossey-Bass.

Appendix C: Scoring and Grading

The purpose of this appendix is to address scoring and grading from the assessment posture described in this book. At the outset, the perspective taken emphasized assessment practices for learning rather than for accountability or selection. As stated in the preface, "Important questions and issues regarding selection and accountability need to be addressed, but not here." This appendix offers some ideas to consider for strengthening connections between assessment information used for learning and accountability. Striking an appropriate balance between the two purposes is desirable. Teacher and student awareness of the difference between assessment information used for these two purposes is a minimal requisite for effective classroom assessment. Students benefit from knowing when information is for accountability purposes, such as grades, and when information is to promote or affirm student learning and competence.

Taking the perspective that grades are not an essential part of assessment for learning does not eliminate legitimate needs for them. We do well, however, to align the grades we give with student skills and knowledge, clearly communicate our grading practices to students and parents, and provide students with as many opportunities as possible to alter grades when their performance warrants it. Assessment as a dynamic process implies that students be afforded opportunities to revise their work, learn from their mistakes, and attain the best grade they can or want to earn.

At the outset, it is well to acknowledge that defining and awarding grades is no easy matter. The important role grades play in decisions about students and the emphasis many attach to grades add to the difficulty of assigning them. The discussion here offers points to consider as you struggle

TABLE C.1 Grade- Versus Competence-Referenced Assessment, Summary Characteristics

Characteristic	*GRA*	*CRA*
Purpose	Accountability/selection	Performance/competence
Primary user(s)	Parents, teachers, students administrators, Institutions	Students
Assessment frequency	Single	Ongoing
Formality	Formal	Formal and informal
Information provided	Summary grade	Affirmation or information about performance

with this professional obligation. As has been suggested for other assessment topics, review of grading practices may lead to maintaining those we now use or modifying them. And, as for other topics, the review of grading practices benefits from discussions with persons knowledgeable about grading practices colleagues, students, parents, and others.

Grade-Versus Competence-Referenced Assessment

Accountability information typically addresses needs of individuals other than the student. Tests used summatively are usually formal in presentation, offered once, yield quantitative scores such as percentage correct, and serve information needs other than the student. Competence-referenced assessment information differs from accountability information in that it is directed at the learner, addresses students' needs for attaining competence, is ongoing, is often somewhat informal, and is exemplified by statements descriptive of the performance, such as "Well done," "Try this," or "This is complete."

Here, summative assessment information is referred to as grade-referenced assessment (GRA); assessment information tied to learning is called competence-referenced assessment (CRA). Differences in information characteristics for these two purposes are listed in Table C.1.

The point of distinguishing between these two assessment perspectives is that each impacts students differently; both assessment purposes have value and should be related. Having students do well on summative tasks that mirror the curriculum is a reasonable goal of instruction and competence-referenced assessment. But one concern about tests developed and used for accountability or selection is to what extent they adequately reflect the curriculum. This concern is particularly acute when tests are designed to rank students in comparison to a group or to force a grade distribution. In such situations, it is advantageous for test developers to use test items at difficulty levels that serve to distribute scores. This situation may result in a mismatch between the test and instruction.

Comparison-based grading procedures sometimes rely on variability on multiple criteria built into test performances, such as time to complete them. When criteria are extraneous to real-world performance standards, such as memorizing formulas, the validity of the test is diminished. Historically, grades evolved to reflect variance in student performances, rooted in the idea that they are distributed as a normal curve. Consequently students' performances are described as well below average, below average, average, above average, or well above average. Attaching a letter designation to each category led to the A-F grading system. It was common that the percentage of students falling in each category was predetermined such that about 10% received As, 20% Bs, 40% Cs, 20% Ds, and 10% Fs. In this scheme, the merit of one's performance depends as much on the performance of others as on one's own—that is, it is a competitive standard. Competitive standards imply that student "competence" is tied to the performance of others. The belief expressed in this book is that students' competence belongs to them.

Grades of D and F were initially established to reflect performances that were below average or substandard defined (usually) in some arbitrary way. From a competence perspective, grades of D and F have limited value. A failing grade is especially damaging if it diminishes students' confidence in their capacity as learners, so necessary for future learning. Use of the grade I rather than F is suggested because earning it is likely due to lack of effort. It is likely that the student who puts forth effort will attain complete performances. Students who make a reasonable effort to engage the curriculum but do not achieve complete performances are in the wrong class or have problems that need to be identified and addressed.

Criteria and Standards

Throughout this book, I have discussed performances in terms of being complete or competent noting that sometimes they are the same. Variance in the quality of performances can result from the criteria applied or standards used with criteria. Marathon races provide an analogy for the multiple criteria and standards that can be applied to performances. Marathons invite runners to "compete" in a race. Most of the competitors do not expect to win; their goal is to complete the 26-mile course. Finishing the race is a complete performance. A significant number of runners will run the course in a time that meets some "respected" competence standard. Finally, a handful of runners will compete to finish first (to win). The runner who finishes first sets the competitive standard. It is noteworthy that in a strictly competitive race, there is no need to keep track of runners' times; a simple rank based on order of finish is sufficient. Similarly, golf may be played either competitively, to see who gets the lowest score, or in relation to some competence standard such as "par."

Grades should reflect student performance and competence as closely as possible. Although teachers are generally obligated to render student grade reports, they exercise considerable control over what grades are given and the criteria on which they are based. Grading practices that clearly spell out performance criteria and standards and give students opportunity to alter their grade are recommended. Establishing such practices can be difficult when school culture factors press for particular grade distributions or in the face of a prevalent viewpoint that too many successful students simply means grading practices are too lenient.

Fundamental to the assessment perspective outlined in this book are complete performances defined by criteria. Beyond this, performance information regarding standards or added criteria may be available to establish grades; omnipresent differences in elements of completed performances can be used as a basis for grades. But all performance components needed for a grade must be clearly communicated to students. Some criteria, such as creativity, although valued, become difficult to describe in a meaningful way. We may encourage creativity and we may acknowledge it, but it is difficult to score or grade.

Competence and understanding sometimes lack precision in definition and do not lend themselves to precise or objective scoring procedures. It is often more difficult to determine a precise score than to recognize a complete performance or a competent one. For example, it is easier to discern student competence in writing when students write papers than when they list the components of an essay. The score may be objective and precise, but the instructional aim is developing student competence in writing. Knowing the components of the essay may be a legitimate instructional outcome, but it is not a substitute for writing. Similarly, the score a student receives may precisely describe his or her knowledge of essay components, but it does not represent student competence in writing.

Grades are summary representations of students' work. One limitation is that grades referenced in terms of variance in student performance usually address the significance of performance differences quantitatively; a grade of B may represent 89% of something whereas the grade A represents 93% of this something. Percentage correct as a summary score is useful to describe performances on singular tasks such as adding two-digit numbers or spelling. The usefulness of percentage correct diminishes when it represents a summary score for complex tasks having multiple components, such as essays, or a summary of multiple activities, such as homework, unit tests, final exams, and class participation. One implication is that an overall summary grade, such as a course grade, does not necessarily reflect student competence directly. With the exception of the student who does everything exceedingly well and earns a high A, grades are likely to represent a summary of performances, some of which may reflect a high level of competence whereas others do not. There is no easy solution to this. From a learning and competence perspective, two complementary suggestions are to ensure that students (and parents) know the inherent limitations of an overall grade and that it reflect the most valued course learnings.

Selected criteria may be included sometimes and not others, or standards may be relaxed for some work. For example, for some products, spelling and punctuation standards may be relaxed. Consistency in the mechanics of writing is valued, but for some purposes exaggerated attention to mechanics may detract from the main intent of the performance. We need to unravel critical performance elements for students. For essential tasks, such as those related to health and safety, or other essential learnings, the requirement is that they be complete and competent, perhaps at a very high performance standard. The implication here is to examine scoring and grading procedures to ensure that they appropriately reflect curricular goals.

An Alternative Perspective on Grading

The grading practices suggested here distinguish between grades or scores awarded for single performances and those that represent a summary of work completed throughout the duration of a course. Keeping single performance grades separate from summary (course) grades is offered as an alternative to adding points achieved on multiple tests and products. The basis for both individual and summary grades are complete performances. Competence is defined in terms of complete performances that represent student knowledge and skills. Course grades represent the aggregate performances achieved by students.

Single Performance Grades

The grade for a single performance informs the student of the level of competence for that particular skill or knowledge topic. Single performances may require criteria and standards that vary. A competent performance may be defined as recalling 80% of a set of facts, such as the names of state capitals, or as including periods at the end of 95% of all sentences.

We improve the validity of grades as performance measures by defining them through student competence. A completed performance (at some specified level) becomes the base "grade" and variance in additional quality elements, clearly specified, becomes the basis for other grades. From the perspective presented in this book, a goal is to establish grade differences that represent qualitatively different performance levels and that differences be apparent to students. So if a C is the base grade, a completed performance, grades of A or B should represent performances that are recognizably, practically, and qualitatively different from the C. The notion is that grading criteria and standards help students perceive competence; they need to know what it is and how to achieve it. Grades that address competence reflect best performance rather than developing performances or typical ones. For this reason, formative assessment information is so important, and grading early drafts, practice tests, or homework designed as practice is counterproductive.

From a student perspective, desirable characteristics of grades are that they

- Are independent of the performance of others
- Provide a valid summary of performances and their quality
- Reflect meaningful performance differences
- Encourage student effort or personal best
- Encourage students to go beyond the curriculum (open ended)

Recommended here are base grades of A, B, C, and I.

A grade of C represents a complete performance.
A grade of B represents competence in important learnings. This grade affirms or acknowledges individual competence.
A grade of A represents competence, consistency, high proficiency, or extended learnings.
The grade of I represents work that does not meet standards for A, B, or C.

These four categories represent base grades. It is a personal option to extend the number of categories in these base ranges to accommodate meaningful variation in performances. But a word of caution is in order here. One goal of this grading posture is to encourage grades that support qualitative rather than quantitative grade distinctions. As a practical matter, quantitative differences will occur; addressing them in the best interests of students is important. Grading single performances depends on whether they are developmental, such as writing, or specified, such as adding two-digit numbers. When a competent performance and a complete or perfect one are the same—counting to 10, for example—a grade is either I or A. When a competent performance is less than a complete or perfect one, such as knowing the state capitals, different standards apply. Here, a grade of C (complete performance) represents a score that is better than chance; a B is awarded for the most important learnings; and an A represents some advanced level, perhaps reflecting only authentic error. The third performance type is when a competent performance is more than a complete one, such as writing. For performances of this type, the notion of a perfect performance is not relevant or is undefined. The grade C represents a complete performance defined in terms of criteria and minimal standards; a grade of B requires a competent performance, clearly defined; and A is for an advanced performance level, again, defined clearly. Performances of this type are developmental and are typically defined using a wide range of completeness and competence. The various grade categories are summarized in Table C.2.

For performances based on objectively scored formats, such as multiple choice tests, a complete performance can be set at some level above a chance

TABLE C.2 Grade Characteristics

Performance	*Example*	*C/Effort*	*B/Proficient*	*A/Competitive*
Competent performance and complete performance are the same	Counting to 10			Performs acceptably
Competent performance is less than a complete one	Knowing the state capitals	Better than chance	Meet established criteria and standards	Meet established high standards (perfect or authentic error) Different criteria applied (e.g., speed)
Competent performance is more than a complete one	Writing a letter	Address criteria, completed work	Meet established criteria and standards	Meet established high standards or extended criteria

score. For example, students completing a 100-item multiple choice test with 4 options for each item would be expected to achieve a score of 25 simply by guessing. Students who correctly answer 35 or 40 of the questions likely know something about the material covered. In other words, students who engage in some purposeful activity in an attempt to learn demonstrate a "complete performance." A performance only a little better than chance is not necessarily a competent one. But it does provide a nonarbitrary point to represent a minimal complete performance. Choosing 70% correct represents a higher minimum (complete) performance level, but is arbitrary in that it could be 50%, 80%, or any other number between zero and 100. The point is to define complete performances in some nonarbitrary (or less arbitrary) way.

Summary Grades: An Alternative Grading Curve

A grading system based on complete performances, competence, effort, and the number and quality of performances attempted is depicted in the grading curve shown in Figure C.1.

Features of this grading curve are that grades depend on the number of tasks attempted, a minimum number of which are specified, and it is implied that they include objectives deemed most important. The number of performances possible is open ended, allowing students to go well beyond the curriculum as defined by "proficient" or competent. The quality of performances also vary by grade, with quality defined by standards or criteria or both. For example, a competitive standard may require students to recall the names of state capitals rather than recognize them. We remember here that recall and recognition are criteria, not standards. Students selecting the competitive standard are encouraged to pursue performance levels that are beyond "proficient."

Standards for performance shown, such as the requirement that at least 80% of performances be at a "proficient" level to receive a grade of B, are illustrative only. Standards for actual use need to be set locally. As mentioned earlier, because the quality of complete performances may vary substantially, it is reasonable to consider adding a plus or minus to the C grade. Similarly, when competence standards are minimal or significantly exceeded, the use of plus and minus may be warranted.

The grading curve described here does not address standards directly. The system encourages everyone to exceed minimal standards, beginning with a complete performance. Beyond a complete performance is competence, meaningfully defined and described in terms of criteria and standards. Beyond competence is the competitive standard. The pinnacle of the competitive standard is perfection. We need to remember, however, that in some instances, a complete performance is the same as a perfect one, for example, counting to 10.

Viewing the purpose of school as promoting student competence in the curriculum suggests that the successful school experience depends on four elements: the number of performances or competencies achieved or attempted, the relative importance of them, the effort required to achieve them, and their quality. Devising a grading system therefore requires classification of the relative importance of instructional aims in the curriculum, description of student performances that address these aims, description of the effort needed to produce them, and establishment of performance quality indicators in terms of criteria and standards. These four elements are then aggregated to derive a summary grade.

Addressing these components is a straightforward activity. The process begins with establishing curriculum priorities in terms of the relative importance of performances and extent of student effort required. Priorities can be coded according to a selected scale, such as 3 being most important, or core, competencies; 2 representing desired competencies; and 1 representing competencies or objectives least essential or that go beyond the curriculum. The scope of the task or effort required to achieve or demonstrate competence in it becomes a second component for weighting performances. Again, a simple scale may differentiate between various levels of effort. An extensive term paper or product that combines multiple objectives is more heavily weighted than a brief quiz covering basic terminology. A third step is to define individual performance quality parameters in terms of criteria and standards. This process is illustrated in the example "Knowing the State Capitals" shown in Appendix D. The values are combined to arrive at a summary grade:

Sample Student Performance Record

Performance	*Priority*	*Scope*	*Quality*	*Percent C*	*Percent B*	*Percent A*
1	3	20	3	20	20	20
2	3	15	3	35	35	35
3	3	10	3	45	45	45
4	3	10	2	55	55	45
5	3	10	3	65	65	55
6	3	10	3	75	75	65
7	3	10	3	85	85	75
8	3	5	2	90	90	75
9	2	5	1	95	90	75
10	1	5	3	100	95	80

This grading system preserves the long-standing belief that there should be a positive relationship between the value of the competence and the effort required to achieve it. At least, objectives that are least valued should not consume the most time.

A modification of this grading scheme is to accumulate performance scores by their combined quality and weight and assign grades using a cutoff score. In the example shown above, there is a total of 300 points possible determined by multiplying the total weight (100) by the highest quality level (3). Eighty percent of the total points would thus be 240, the level required for an A, or top grade. The grade of B would be based on 80% of the second quality level (2). Consistent work at this level would result in 200 points. Eighty percent would be 160 points. Finally, the aggregate total of completed work would be 100 points, 80% of which would be 80 points. An added requirement for any grade might be to complete 80% of the core performances.

Individual performance records should contain information about performances in terms of the appropriate criteria. Some performance summaries, such as knowing the state capitals, are best described by simply indicating a percentage correct. Where multiple criteria are used, information that describes performance in terms of the criteria are useful. One advantage of rubrics is the information they convey to students. Assigning numbers to rubric categories yield scores that can be used for grades.

One benefit of a collective performance grading system and format is to allow a student profile in terms of competencies. Such profiles can help students (and teachers) identify and keep track of learning and communicate

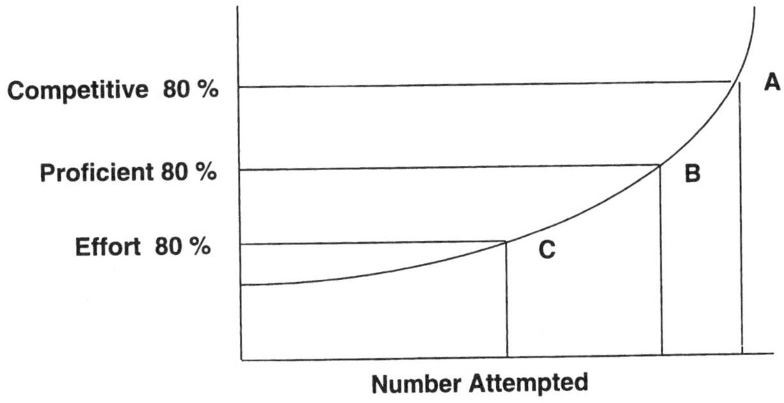

Figure C.1. Grading Schematic

descriptive information to parents. The system also allows aggregation of class data in terms of learning progress for use by teacher.

Concluding Comments

When we view schooling as promoting competence, we need a reward system for growth and progress that stands alongside the one for competence and proficiency. Grades of B or C may connote an excellent effort and indicate substantial learning. Students benefit from experiencing a complete performance even if it is a marginal one. Sufficiency is a valued precursor to proficiency. A complete performance of a skill previously absent is worthy of affirmation. Teachers also benefit by attending to effort and progress because their job is to facilitate learning and student competence.

In several chapters, the quality of work and the pace of instruction were discussed in the context of effective students. One implication of that discussion is that the quality of work is influenced by, among other things, the pace of instruction. One purpose of a curriculum review is to prioritize learning goals to reduce the breadth of content coverage in favor of depth (competence). Identified important learnings that attend a leaner curriculum can strengthen connections between students' effort and their performance. At the same time, encouraging students to expand their competence beyond expressed content and performance standards is recommended.

Appendix D: Examples of Assessment: Knowing the State Capitals

A frequent objective for students is to know the state capitals. Knowing them represents a complete performance that students can recognize. Students may be asked to demonstrate their knowledge by matching capitals with states or responding to a series of multiple choice questions that include the correct city along with three or four that are incorrect. These formats require recognition. Alternatively, we may ask students to supply correct capital cities by writing them next to a list of the states. This assessment performance requires recall. Additional criteria may be to correctly spell the name of each city or to locate it on a map.

Asking students to recall capitals requires a different and more time consuming level of knowing than having them match or recognize correct capital cities. As a complete performance, knowing the state capitals treats each city equally. We might thus score the performance by giving two points for each capital, resulting in a perfect score of 100. In addition, we might set a passing score of 70%, meaning that a student must "know" 35 of the 50 state capitals to receive a passing score. Allowing for authentic error, we set an A at 94%, or 47 correctly named capitals. A grade of B is set at 85% to 93% (42 to 46 correct), a C includes 75% to 84% (38 to 41 correct), and a D grade is given for correctly naming 36 or 37 of the 50 capitals.

An alternative scoring procedure, based on a the same complete performance, reflects the importance or value attached to knowing each of the 50 capitals. A competent performance is thus altered from the one described above.

Point Groupings	*Number*	*Points*	*Cumulative Points*
Home state (10 points/recall)	1 @ 10	10	10
Bordering states (5 points/recall)	4 @ 5	20	30
Most populous states (3 points/ recognize)	20 @ 3	45	75
Remaining states (2 points/recognize)	25 @ 1	25	100

In this scoring scheme, students can get a C by knowing 25 state capitals, including their state of residence, four bordering states, and the 20 most populous. The requirements for an A are modified to require only 45 correct, as long as these include the home state, bordering states, and the most populous states. The requirements for a B change in that the grade can be achieved by knowing only 35 of the 50 capitals. A passing score requires "knowing" at least 23 correctly identified capitals.

References

Airasian, P. W. (1994). *Classroom assessment* (2nd ed.). New York: McGraw-Hill.

American Association for the Advancement of Science. (1993). *Benchmarks for science literacy.* New York: Oxford University Press.

Bloom, B. S., Englehart, M. D., Furst, E. J., Hill, W. H., & Krathwohl, D. R. (Eds.). (1956). *Taxonomy of educational objectives. Handbook 1: Cognitive domain.* New York: David McKay.

Gullickson, A. R. (1986). Teacher education and teacher-perceived needs in educational measurement and evaluation. *Journal of Educational Measurement, 23,* 355-368.

Gullickson, A. R. (1993). Matching measurement instruction to classroom-based evaluation: Perceived discrepancies, needs, and challenges. In S. L. Wise & J. C. Conoley (Eds.), *Teacher training in measurement and assessment skills.* Lincoln: Buros Institute of Mental Measurements, University of Nebraska.

Joint Committee on Standards for Educational Evaluation, Daniel L. Stufflebeam, Chair. (1988). *Standards for the evaluation of educational personnel.* Newbury Park, CA: Sage.

Linn, R. L., & Gronlund, N. E. (1995). *Measurement and assessment in teaching* (7th ed.). Englewood Cliffs, NJ: Merrill.

Merriam Webster's collegiate dictionary (10th ed.). (1993). Springfield, MA: Merriam Webster.

National Commission on Excellence in Education. (1983.) *A nation at risk: The imperative for educational reform.* Washington, DC: Author.

National Council of Teachers of Mathematics. (1989). *Curricular and evaluation standards for school mathematics.*

Noel, J. V. (1962). *Division officer's guide* (5th ed.). Annapolis, MD: U.S. Naval Institute.

Saint-Exupéry, A. de. (1943). *The little prince.* New York: Harcourt, Brace & World.

Scriven, M. (1991). *Evaluation thesaurus* (4th ed.). Newbury Park, CA: Sage.

Stiggins, R. J. (1994). *Student-centered classroom assessment.* New York: Merrill.

Walberg, H. J. (1984, May). Improving productivity of America's schools. *Educational Leadership,* pp. 19-27.

Wiggins, G. P. (1993). *Assessing student performance.* San Francisco: Jossey-Bass.

Willson, V. (Ed.). (1989). *Academic achievement and aptitude testing.* Austin, TX: ProEd.